Training Guide
Windows 95

Dexter J Booth

Addison Wesley Longman Limited
Edinburgh Gate, Harlow
Essex CM20 2JE, England
and Associated Companies throughout the world

© Addison Wesley Longman Limited 1996

Screen shots reprinted with permission from Microsoft Corporation

The right of Dexter J Booth to be identified as author of this Work has been asserted by him in accordance with the Copyright, Designs and Patents Act 1988

All rights reserved; no part of this publication may be reproduced, stored in any retrieval system, or transmitted in any form or by any means, electronic, mechanical, photocopying, recording, or otherwise without either the prior written permission of the Publishers or a licence permitting restricted copying in the United Kingdom issued by the Copyright Licensing Agency Ltd, 90 Tottenham Court Road, London W1P 9HE.

First published 1996

British Library Cataloguing in Publication Data
A catalogue entry for this title is available from the British Library

ISBN 0-582-29776-1

Printed and bound in Great Britain by Henry Ling Ltd,
at the Dorset Press, Dorchester, Dorset

Contents

Introduction v

Getting Started vii

Section A   **First steps into Windows 95**   **1**
- Task 1   Window manipulation 2
- Task 2   Fun and games 7
- Task 3   Playing Minesweeper and Solitaire simultaneously 13
- Task 4   The Desktop icons 14
- Task 5   The Recycle bin 19
- Task 6   The Task bar 21

Section B   **The Start button options**   **25**
- Task 7   Accessories 26
- Task 8   The WordPad accessory 29
- Task 9   Creating a document in WordPad 37
- Task 10   Printing a document 41
- Task 11   Starting to use the Paint accessory 43
- Task 12   The Paint accessory in detail 47
- Task 13   Drawing a diagram 51
- Task 14   Using Paint to enhance a WordPad document 56
- Task 15   Placing an Object into a document 58

Section C   **File management**   **63**
- Task 16   The Windows 95 Explorer 64
- Task 17   Accessing files from Explorer 71
- Task 18   Moving files from folder to folder 76
- Task 19   Manipulating Help 80
- Task 20   Find 87
- Task 21   Backing up, restoring and comparing files 92

Section D   **Advanced features**   **99**
- Task 22   Customizing the display 100
- Task 23   Password protection 109
- Task 24   Keyboard and mouse settings 112
- Task 25   Accessibility options 119
- Task 26   Installing Microsoft Excel 5.0 124

Glossary 127

Index 131

Introduction

Microsoft® Windows® 95 is Microsoft's latest version of their *graphical user interface* (GUI for short and pronounced *gooey*). A *user interface* is what you the user experiences when you are operating a computer. It comprises not just the visual aspect of what is displayed on the computer monitor screen but also the way you interact with the computer to instruct it to perform whatever task you wish it to perform; it deals with both the visual aspect and the 'feel' of the machine. Working with a computer involves as much the mind-set of the user as it involves the user's physical actions. Ideally, the user should be able to think of what he or she desires the computer to do and then be able to instruct the machine to do it in the most natural manner possible.

Learning how to use a computer is, in many ways, very like learning to ride a bike. Learning to ride a bike requires you to think of everything you are doing; sitting on the saddle, holding the handle bars in the right position, turning the pedals whilst keeping your balance and watching where you are going. The upshot is that you keep falling off because your mind is trying to do too many things all at the same time. When you have learned how to ride then sitting in the saddle, steering, pedalling and maintaining a balance come naturally and all you need to concentrate on is where you are going; the bike becomes a familiar environment within which you travel from here to there.

The computer is very like this. At first there is so much going on it becomes impossible to keep a track of everything. How did I get here? Where was I before I pushed that key? How am I going to open the Wordprocessor? What was I supposed to do when that message appeared? Why am I going crazy? I shall never be able to use one of these things! Pretty soon, however, with a little perseverance you find that you begin to become more comfortable with the system. You stop worrying about navigating your way around the system – you just do it. If you take a wrong turn – so what, go back and start again. Eventually, the user interface becomes an environment within which you work and within which you instruct the computer to perform all the necessary tasks relevant to your job in hand.

And this is where the *graphical* bit comes in. I don't know of anyone who thinks in terms of words strung together in the form of sentences and whole paragraphs. Everyone I know thinks in terms of pictures. Ask anyone how they enjoyed their last holiday and their eyes temporarily glaze as they picture themselves lying back in the warm sunshine (or rain if your holiday was in the Western Isles). So it makes sense to create the user interface in the form of pictures or graphics – a graphical user interface – where every graphic, or picture conveys an impression pertinent to the graphic's particular purpose.

Windows 95 can be installed either by itself or as an update to a previously installed copy of Windows 3.1. The latter enables Windows 95 to access a number of features provided by Windows 3.1 but not by

Windows 95. Consequently, as you rove through Windows 95 you may find that the appearance of your version of Windows 95 differs slightly from that given in the *Guide* where it is assumed that no pre-existing version of Windows 3.1 has been installed. However, the essential features presented here will all be there.

For the further purposes of this *Guide* it will be assumed that Windows 95 has already been installed onto your computer. Furthermore, it is also assumed that all you need to do to find yourself within the environment of the graphical user interface of Windows 95 is to switch the computer on and wait for the Windows 95 opening screen to appear.

Getting started

Entering Windows 95

Switch your computer on and wait for the Windows 95 screen display to appear:

The display covers the entire monitor screen and what you see is referred to as the *desktop*. Its quite a natural name to give it; everything you do from now on will be done from this desktop. Your display may not look exactly like this one but the essential features will be there.

There are three essential features in this display. Somewhere on the screen you will see an arrow pointing upwards and to the left.

Using the mouse

At the side of your computer, next to the keyboard, is the mouse, a small box with a roller ball beneath it and some buttons on the top. Grip the mouse, push it backwards, forwards and sideways over the worksurface whilst watching the arrow move on the screen. Very quickly you instinctively link the gearing and direction of motion of the mouse with the equivalent motion of the arrow. The arrow is called the *pointer* because it enables you to use the mouse to point at any chosen screen location. It is also sometimes referred to as the *cursor* after the Latin verb *currere* which means to run. So we call this little graphic the pointer because that is what it does or we call it the cursor because that is how it does it.

Icons

Down the left-hand side of the screen are a number of small pictures, each one with a name underneath it. These pictures, like all such pictures that you will come to see are called *icons* and they represent gateways from the desktop to various facilities offered by the system. We shall say no more now of these, instead we defer a discussion to later in the book.

Task bar At the bottom of the display is a bar called the *Task* bar that runs the width of the screen with the word **Start** in the left-hand corner. This is not unlike what happened to Lewis Carrol's Alice who, after falling down the rabbit hole, found a bottle with **Drink Me** written on the label. Alice did just that and suddenly began to shrink. However, there the similarity ends.

Look closely at that word Start – it is surrounded by a rectangle. We call the rectangle a *button* and this particular button is called the *Start button*. Buttons are there to be pressed but how do we press this one?

On the top of your mouse are two, or maybe three butttons; we shall be concerned only with the left-hand button at the moment. Move the pointer across the desktop until it is pointing at the Start button then press the left-hand mouse button and release it. Instantly, a list appears:

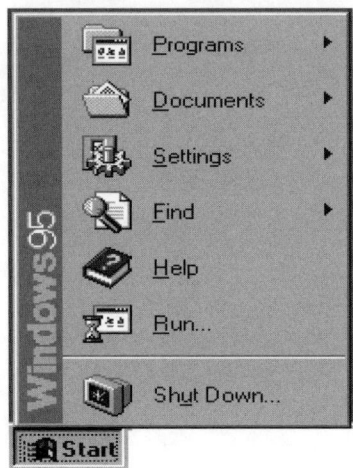

What you have just done is to *press* the Start button by pointing to it and then *pressing* or *clicking* the mouse button. In future we shall refer to this action as clicking the Start button rather than pressing the Start button. The effect of clicking the Start button is to open up a list of further options. Such a list of options is called a *menu* of options; in this case it is the Start menu

Menu options Move the pointer up and down this menu of options and you will see a dark contrasting stripe appear over the particular option you are pointing at.

Point at the option called **Programs** at the top of the menu and a second menu of further options appears:

Now point at **Accessories** at the top of this second menu and yet another menu appears:

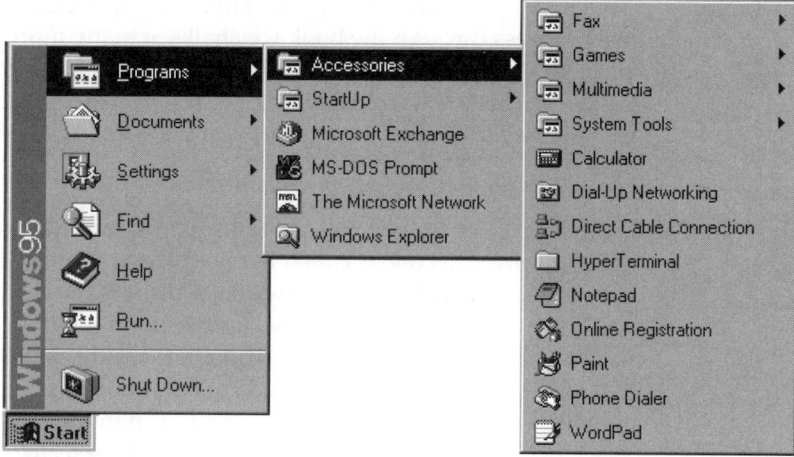

Move the cursor and point at **Games** in this third menu and a fourth menu opens; just like a Russian doll – lists within lists within lists.

Now point at **Settings** in the Start menu just beneath the Documents option and all the other menus close to reveal a menu emanating from Settings:

Another list within a list. Only those options in a menu with an *arrowhead* to the right will contain a further menu – this is why the arrowhead is there, to inform you of the fact. Point at **Shut Down** at the bottom of the Start menu that emanates from the Start button. Now click the mouse button. A rectangular area opens in the centre of the screen:

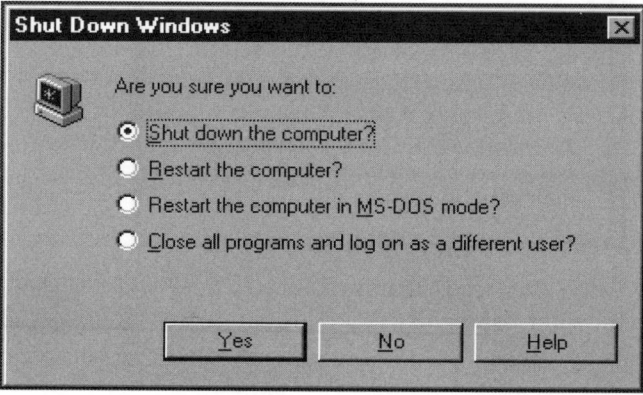

Getting started **ix**

Dialog boxes	This rectangular area is a special kind of *window* called a *dialog box*. As we progress through the book we shall see many more windows, not all of them looking exactly like this but all of them having certain common features. This one is called a dialog box because it is requesting an answer to a question – it requires you the user to put some information into it.

Window features	At the top of every window is a Title bar on which is written the name of the window. This one is called the Shut Down Windows window. To the far right-hand end is a cross – we shall discuss the cross in a moment. In the body of the window is a question beneath which are four circular *radio buttons* each with an annotation to the right. The top radio button has a black dot in its centre to indicate that this has been selected by default. Point to and click each radio button in turn. As you do so the black dot moves to the radio button you have selected.

Remember: Radio buttons permit a single choice to made from a list of options.

At the bottom of the dialog box are three more buttons. If you were to click the **Yes** button then you would be answering the question posed by affirming the selection that had been made via the radio buttons. If you were to click the **No** button then you would be answering the question posed by denying the selection you had made and the window would close.

Help	Confused? Click the **Help** button and immediately a Help window opens:

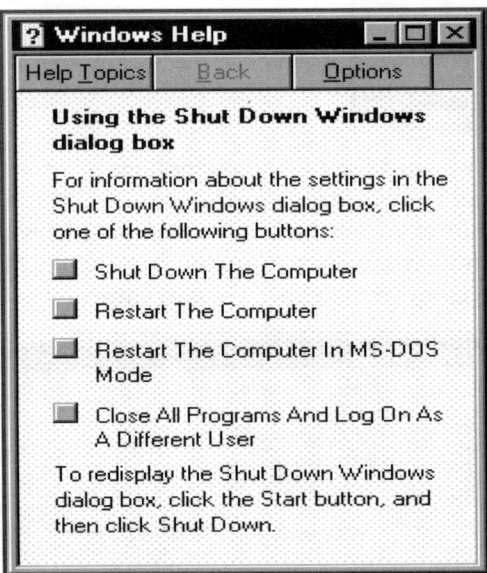

Before you read the information in the Windows Help window look at the right-hand end of the Title bar in the Windows Help window.

There is the cross along with two other symbols – icons all three.

Click the middle icon and the Help window expands to fill the entire screen. Look again at that middle icon it has changed. Click the middle icon again and the window shrinks to its original size. Just like Alice. The middle icon that you see now is called the Maximize button because when you click it the window takes on its maximum size. When this happens the Maximize button changes to a Restore button and clicking the Restore button restores the window to its original size.

Click the left-hand icon of the three and the window disappears. It has not gone altogether because if you look at the Task bar at the bottom of the screen you will see the the window has been shrunk to its button icon and placed on the Task bar. The button you clicked is called the Minimize button - it enables the window to be reduced in size to a small icon on the Task bar. Now you understand why the Task bar is so named; it retains the icons of all those tasks that are still active.

Click the **Windows Help** button on the task bar and the Windows Help window re-appears. In each of these three stages, full screen, small window and button icon the window is still open – it is just a different size in each case. Keep repeating this sequence until you are happy that you understand exactly what is going on here.

Closing a window

Now the cross. Click the cross at the top right-hand corner of the Title bar of the Windows Help window and the window disappears. No icon on the Task bar, nothing. You have just closed the window. The cross is called the window's **Close** button.

Wait a minute. We did not read what was written in the Help window. Re-open the Help window associated with the Shut Down option and read the information that it contains:

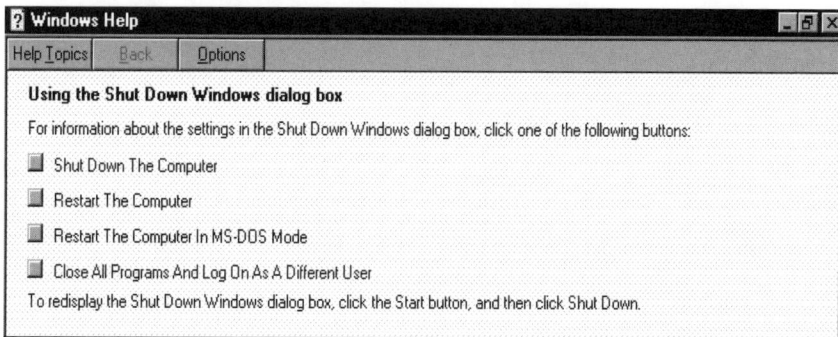

In the body of the Help window are four buttons. When you point at each button in turn the arrow pointer turns into a pointing finger – that really is a pointer. There is a purpose in this. The pointing finger indicates that there is more to see. Point at each of these buttons in turn and click the mouse button to reveal a box containing further information.

Close the Windows Help window and ensure that the Shut Down Windows window is open.

Getting started **xi**

Leaving Windows 95

Just one further bit of information. In the Shut Down Windows window select the first option by clicking the first of the four radio buttons.

Click the **Yes** button and the shut down procedure is activated causing you to leave Windows 95.

Summary

What have you learned?

- The graphical user interface consists of pictures or graphics called icons that can be pointed to by moving the mouse to move the pointer to the appropriate location on the screen.

- The opening screen of Windows 95 is called the desktop and on the desktop is a collection of icons. At the bottom of the desktop is the Task bar which displays the Start button.

- Buttons are made to be pressed and this is achieved by pointing at them and clicking the left-hand mouse button. This is called clicking a button.

- Sometimes clicking a button reveals a choice (a menu) of further options each one of which can be selected by pointing to the option and clicking the mouse button – we call this clicking the option.

- Windows are rectangular areas of the screen. Each window has a Title bar and a Close button. Some windows also have Maximize and Minimize buttons.

Now you are ready to explore all the features of Windows 95.

Section A

First steps into Windows 95

In this Section you will be introduced to the basic features of the Windows 95 environment and the use of the mouse.

By playing the games Solitaire and Minesweeper you will learn how to:

- manipulate the screen pointer
- select options by pointing and clicking
- move graphics by dragging
- re-size windows by dragging

In addition, you will become familiar with the overall desktop display and be able to recognize specific features of the display.

Task 1:   Window manipulation
Task 2:   Fun and games
Task 3:   Playing Minesweeper and Solitaire simultaneously
Task 4:   The Desktop icons
Task 5:   The Recycle bin
Task 6:   The Task bar

| Task 1 | # Window manipulation

> ➤ **Accessing applications from menus and manipulating windows and icons with the mouse.**

Ensure that the Windows 95 Desktop is on display.

Activity 1.1 **Opening the Solitaire window**

1 CLICK the **Start** button to reveal a menu of further options.

2 POINT at the **Programs** option to reveal a second menu of further options.

3 POINT at the **Accessories** option to reveal a third menu of further options.

4 POINT at the **Games** option to reveal a fourth and final menu of options.

5 SELECT the **Solitaire** option by clicking the **Solitaire** icon to reveal the **Solitaire** window.

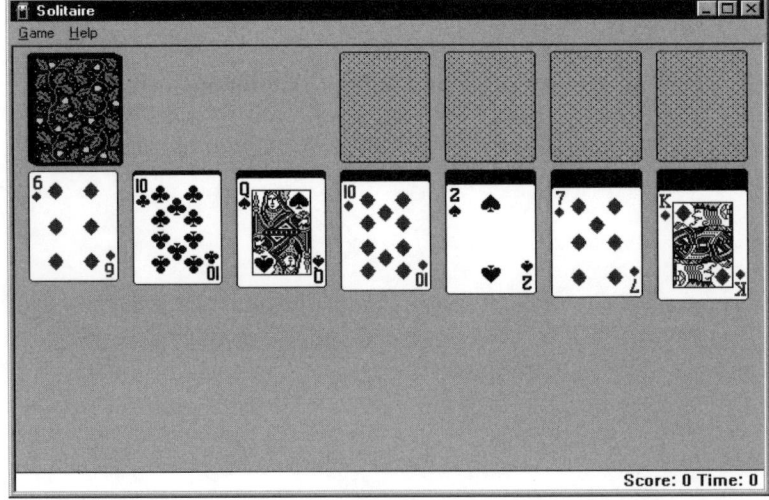

This window has a Title bar – carrying the name Solitaire and the three window sizing buttons at the right-hand end. Beneath the Title bar is a *Menu bar* containing the two words **Game** and **Help**. These words are called *commands* and each one represents an access point to further options concerned with the contents of the window, in this case, the game of Solitaire.

Activity 1.2 **Using the commands on the Menu bar**

1 CLICK the command **Game** on the Solitaire window Menu bar to reveal a drop-down menu of further options:

2 CLICK the **Options...** option to reveal the **Options** dialog box:

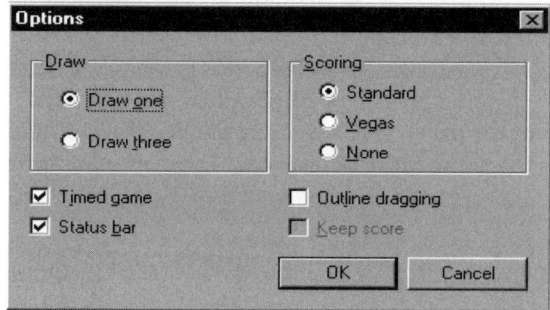

3 CLICK the appropriate radio buttons and *check boxes* (the small square boxes) to ensure that the contents of the dialog box match those of the above illustration.

Whereas only one radio button in a list of radio buttons can be selected, in a list of check boxes more than one of the list can be selected. A check box either displays a tick to show that it has been selected or it displays nothing to show that it has not been selected. The selections that you have chosen will dictate the style of the Solitaire game that you will play.

4 CLICK the **OK** button to close the **Options** dialog box.

The Solitaire window only covers part of the screen. We require it to be larger but not to fill the entire screen.

Activity 1.3 **Moving and re-sizing the Solitaire window**

1 POINT at the Title bar, depress and hold down the left-hand mouse button and move the mouse across the worksurface.

The Solitaire window moves in response to the movement of the mouse. This is called *dragging* and every window can be dragged in this way.

2 DRAG the window so that its top left-hand corner coincides with the top left-hand corner of the monitor screen and then release the mouse button.

3 POINT at the right-hand edge of the window and you will notice that the pointer changes to a double-headed horizontal arrow. You may have to use a little delicacy with the mouse to catch this effect.

4   With the double-headed arrow on display DRAG the edge of the Solitaire window towards the right-hand edge of the monitor screen leaving about 3 cm of desktop showing and then release the mouse button.

The same can be done to increase or decrease the depth of the Solitaire window by dragging the bottom of the window. Then the double-headed arrow is vertical. Similarly, the corners of the window can be dragged with the inclined double-headed arrow which appears when you point at a corner of the window.

5   RE-SIZE the **Solitaire** window until the monitor screen displays a 3 cm border of the desktop to the right and below the Solitaire window.

The purpose of the window is to display the effects of a specific application. Here the application is the game of Solitaire. One of the great advantages of the Windows 95 GUI is that different windows can be open at the same time thereby enabling different applications to be run simultaneously.

6   With the Solitare window still open repeat the instructions of *Activity 1.1* and OPEN the **Minesweeper** game window:

7   DRAG the **Minesweeper** window so that its bottom right-hand corner coincides with the bottom right-hand corner of the monitor screen.

The Minesweeper window appears in front of the Solitaire window. Notice the Task bar. To the right of the start button are two buttons labelled Solitaire and Minesweeper but whereas the Minesweeper button appears depressed the Solitaire button does not.

Activity 1.4   Switching between applications

1   CLICK the **Solitaire** button on the Task bar.

Immediately the Solitaire window comes to the fore in front of the Minesweeper window.

2   CLICK anywhere on the visible part of the Minesweeper window and immediately the Minesweeper window comes to the fore.

In this way it is possible to switch between applications

3 OPEN the **FreeCell** games window and see the effect of switching between applications either by clicking the appropriate buttons on the Task bar or by clicking the appropriate window.

Activity 1.5 Closing a window

Ensure that the Solitaire window is in front of the other two windows.

1 CLICK the cross (the Close button) to the far right of the Title bar.

The Solitaire window closes and its button disappears from the Task bar. The Solitaire game is no longer – it has been closed down. Ensure that the Minesweeper window is on display in front of the FreeCell window.

2 CLICK the **Mine** icon to the far left of the Title bar to reveal a drop-down menu of further options:

This menu of options provides an alternative collection of window manipulation tools.

3 CLICK the **Close** option and the window closes.

This has the same effect as clicking the Close button at the other end of the Title bar.

4 CLICK the **FreeCell** icon to the far left of the FreeCell window Title bar to reveal the same drop-down menu of commands.

You will notice that after the word Close is the cryptic message:

Alt-F4

This is the equivalent keyboard command.

5 CLICK the body of the FreeCell window and the drop-down menu closes.

6 On the keyboard PRESS and hold down the **Alt** key.

7 PRESS the **F4** function key and the FreeCell window closes.

This is a third method of closing a window. Indeed, it is possible to operate within Windows 95 without using a mouse but using the keyboard instead. However, the use of a mouse is intrinsic to the spirit of the graphical user interface because keyboard commands need to be memorized whereas the use of a mouse eliminates that need. For this reason keyboard commands will not be mentioned in this *Guide* unless they contribute significantly to the ease of use of the system.

| Task 2 | Fun and games

> **Gaining practice and familiarity with the mouse and manipulating applications.**

Ensure that the desktop is on display and that no other windows are open.

Activity 2.1 **Playing the game of Solitaire**

1 OPEN the **Solitaire** window and DRAG the window until its top left-hand corner is coincident with the top left-hand corner of the monitor screen. RE-SIZE the window until there is a 3 cm border of desktop visible to the right of and below the window.

2 CLICK the **Maximize** button so that the Solitaire window fills the entire monitor screen above the Task bar.

Re-locating and re-sizing the window was not a waste of time because when you click the restore button the window will shrink to its previous location and size. Try it.

3 CLICK the **Game** command on the Menu bar and SELECT the **Options...** option.

4 By activating the appropriate radio button and check boxes in the Options dialog box ensure that:

Draw One is selected in the Draw box
Standard is selected in the Scoring box
Timed Game and **Status Bar** are both checked
Outline dragging is not checked

5 CLICK the **OK** button to close the Options dialog box.

6 CLICK the **Game** command on the Menu bar again and this time SELECT the **Deck...** option to reveal a dialog box displaying twelve different card backs:

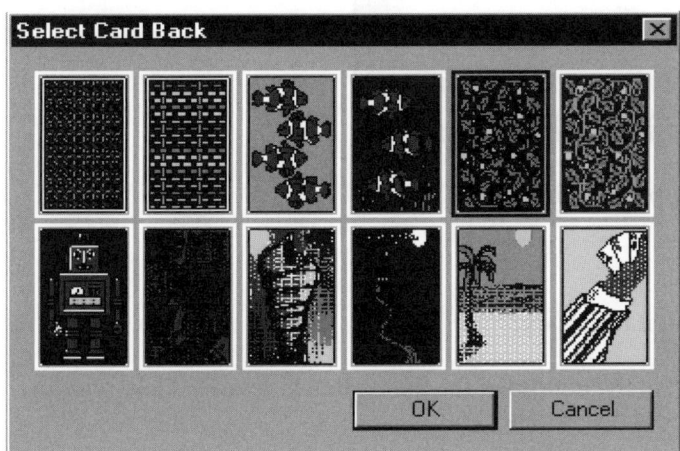

7 CLICK a card back that is different to the one currently being used in the Solitaire window.

8 CLICK the **OK** button and you will notice that the card back in the Solitaire window changes to the one just selected.

9 CLICK the **Game** command on the Menu bar yet again and this time SELECT the **Deal** option.

Immediately the cards are re-dealt. This is very useful if you find that the game you are playing is not going to work out and you would like to start afresh with a new deal.

We shall assume that you are not familiar with the rules of Solitaire patience and for such a player as you there is an on-line Help facility available.

Activity 2.2   Using the Help facility

1 CLICK the **Help** command on the Menu bar of the Solitaire window to reveal a drop-down menu of further options.

2 SELECT the **Help Topic** option to reveal the Solitaire Help dialog box:

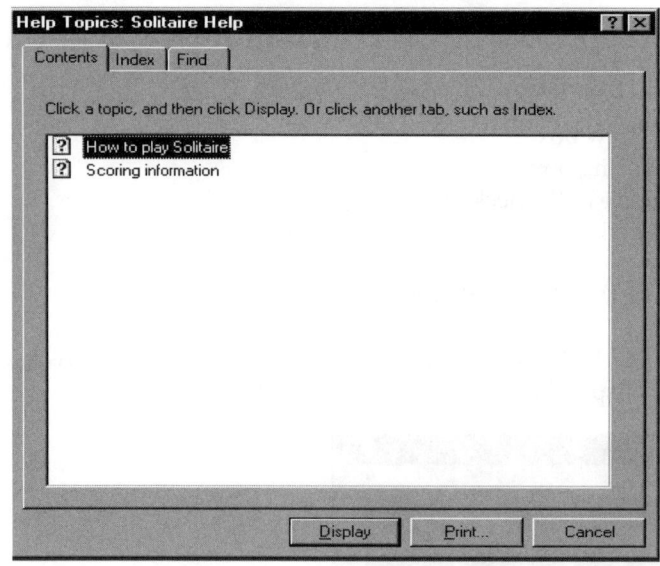

3 ENSURE that of the two topics the first one

   How to play Solitaire

   is highlighted by clicking it if necessary.

4 CLICK the **Display** button at the bottom of the dialog box to reveal a Help window that contains the rules of Solitaire patience.

8 First steps into Windows 95

Read the rules and you will see mention of double-clicking. We shall discuss this a little later.

Now, yet another way to close a window.

5 On the keyboard PRESS the **Esc** key and the Help window closes.

This method does not work with all windows. For instance the Solitaire window will not close using this method. Try it.

If you are still unsure of how to play Solitaire here are the rules:

The Rules of Solitaire Patience
From the seven dealt piles of cards the play proceeds by placing a face-up card in one pile on top of another face-up card in another pile. The rule that governs this states that the card placed on top must be one point below the card underneath and of the opposite colour. When a card is moved to another position, if it reveals a face-down card then that card must be turned over.

If none of the revealed cards can be moved then the top card of the top left-hand stack is turned over and, if possible, placed on on one of the seven piles.

If the last card in a column is moved to leave an empty column then the column can be re-opened by placing a King at the top of the column. No more than seven columns are permitted.

If an Ace is revealed then that is placed face-up in one of the four reserved locations in the right-hand side of the top row. If an Ace is displayed in the top row then the Two of the same suit can be placed face-up on top of it. The Three of the same suit can then be placed on the Two and so on until the complete suit up to the King is stacked together. The object of the game is to build up the four suits of cards in this way.

Cards are moved on the screen by dragging them and cards are turned over when required by clicking them.

Activity 2.3   Moving a card

1 POINT to any face-up card and drag it to any other face-up card. When you release the mouse button one of two events occur:

Either the move is a legal move in which case the card remains where it has been put or the move is an illegal move in which case the card floats back to its original position.

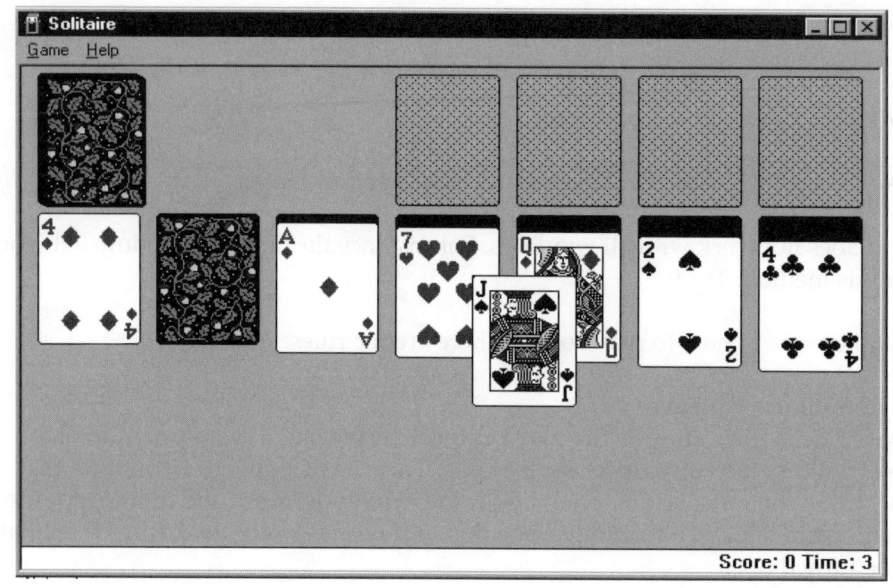

Activity 2.4 Starting the play

Look around to see if any card can be moved on top of any other. Remember one point less in value and opposite colour. If you can make a legal move you will expose the card underneath which is face-down.

1 CLICK the face-down card to turn it over.

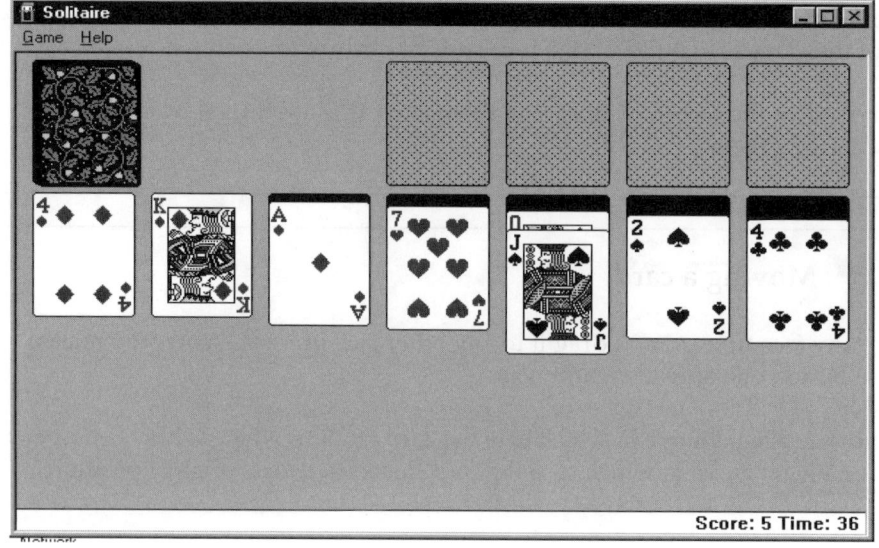

2 REPEAT this procedure until no further card can be moved.

Activity 2.5 **Double clicking**

If an Ace is revealed then this is dragged to one of the four reserved locations on the left of the top row. An alternative method of moving it there is to *double-click* the card.

1 To double-click an Ace, POINT at the card and then PRESS and RELEASE the mouse button twice in quick succession.

The Ace immediately floats into position.

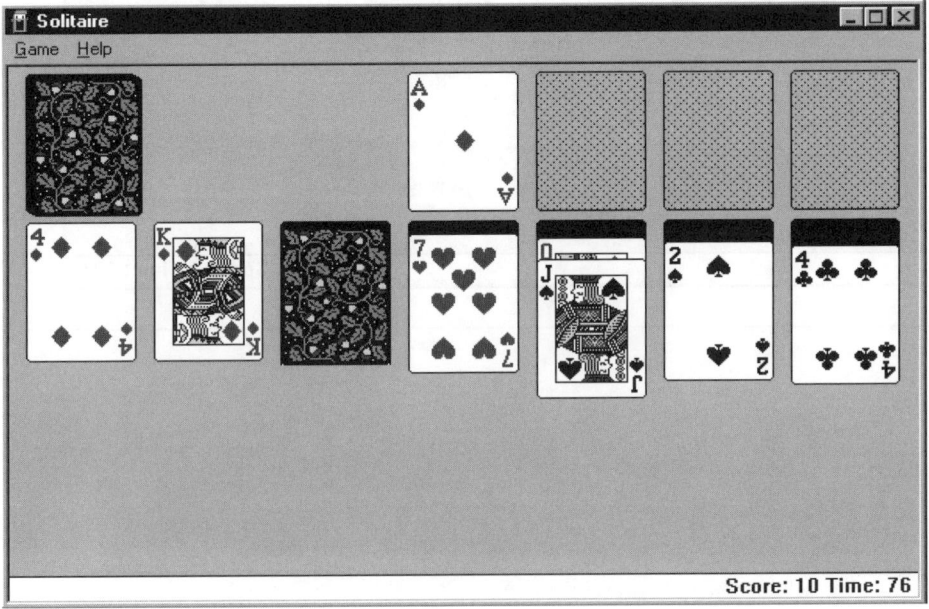

Activity 2.6 **Revealing the stack**

When no further cards can be moved amongst the seven piles we must reveal the top card of the stack in the top left-hand corner of the window.

1 CLICK the top card and it turns over. Can you move this one onto one of the seven piles? If you can, then move it. If you cannot then turn over the top card of the stack again.

Fun and games 11

Task 3	# Playing Minesweeper and Solitaire simultaneously

> ➤ **Demonstrating the ability of Windows 95 to run more than one application at the same time.**

Ensure that the Solitaire window is open and located with its top left-hand corner coincident with the top left-hand corner of the monitor screen and with a 3 cm border around the left-hand edge and the bottom.

Activity 3.1 **The game Minesweeper**

1 OPEN the **Minesweeper** window via the Start button on the Task bar.

2 DRAG the **Minesweeper** window until its bottom right-hand corner is coincident with the bottom right-hand corner of the monitor screen

Hidden beneath the tiling of the Minesweeper board are a number of mines. A tile is *removed* by clicking it using the usual left-hand mouse button and a square is *marked* by clicking it using the right-hand mouse button. A marked tile displays a small flag and cannot be removed until it is unmarked by clicking again with the right-hand mouse button. The purpose of the game is to locate all the mines as quickly as possible by removing every tile that does not cover a mine and marking every tile that does cover a mine. If a tile is removed that does cover a mine the game ends. If a removed tile reveals a number then that is the number of mines located somewhere within the eight tiles that surround the number. The number of hidden mines is given by the display at the top left of the Minesweeper window and the display top right records the time you have taken in seconds.

3 PLAY the game of Minesweeper.

4 CLICK the **Solitaire** window to make it the active window and start a game of Solitaire.

Keep playing until you succeed and obtain the collection of cascading cards. When this happens:

5 CLICK the **Minesweeper** window and play a game of Minesweeper.

You will find that as you play the board game the Solitaire cascade continues in the window behind. It would appear that the computer has two independent application running simultaneously. What is actually happening is that the computer is switching its attention from one application to another at such a rapid rate that it gives the illusion of the two applications running simultaneously.

| Task 4 | The desktop icons

➤ **The role of the desktop as a storage space for application icons**

Enter Windows 95 and ensure that the desktop is on display:

Activity 4.1 **The desktop features**

The desktop display consists of a large area at the top of the screen on which are located a number of icons. Because the desktop is used to store icons your screen display will, in all probability, not look identically the same. However, the basic features will be the same and at least three of the icons should be there; the My Computer icon, the Briefcase icon and the Recycle Bin icon.

1   DOUBLE-CLICK the **My Computer** icon.

Immediately the My Computer window opens. Inside this window is a further collection of icons, one of which is called Control Panel:

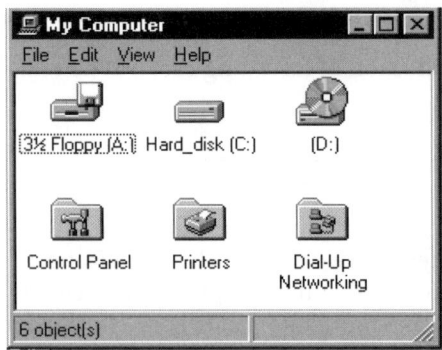

2   DOUBLE-CLICK the **Control Panel** icon to reveal the Control Panel window:

14 First steps into Windows 95

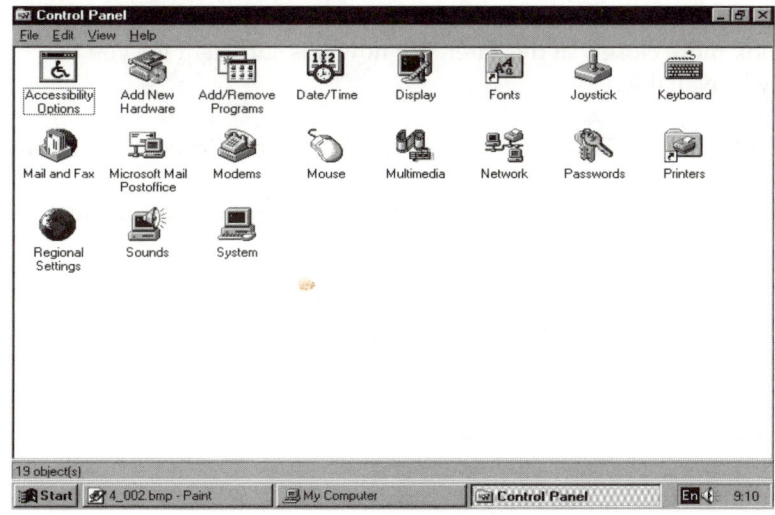

Again, we see that this window contains yet another collection of icons. Each of these icons represents an access point to some facility that governs the control of both Windows 95 and the very computer itself. Furthermore, an icon is *opened up* by double-clicking it.

We shall not concern ourselves at the moment with the details of which facility each of the icons in the Control Panel represents. Instead, we shall demonstrate how we can take advantage of the storage capability of the desktop.

Activity 4.2   **Placing a Shortcut icon on the desktop**

1   ENSURE that the Control Panel window is on display.

One of the icons in this window is called **Date/Time**.

2   DOUBLE-CLICK the **Date/Time** icon to reveal the Date/Time Properties window:

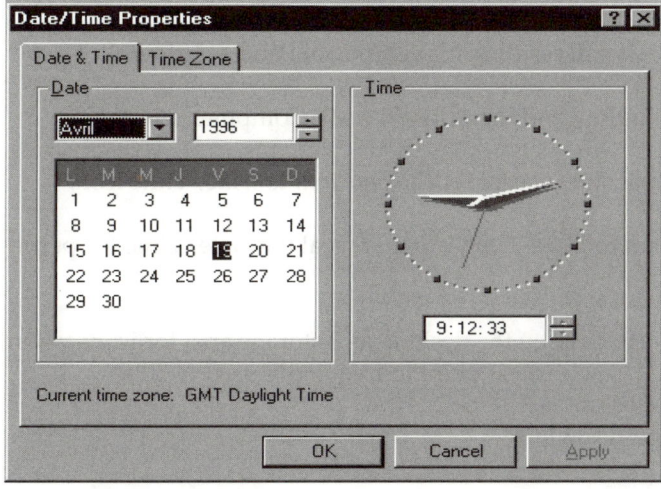

The desktop icons 15

This window permits us to re-set the time and date that is currently recorded by the computer. We shall look more closely at this later. For now it is sufficient for you to realize that the facility is available.

3 CLICK the **Close** button on the Title bar and close the Date/Time Properties window.

You will notice that the window has shrunk back to its icon inside the Control Panel window.

We shall now assume that in future we are going to make frequent use of the Date & Time facility. To avoid having to remember that to access it we must travel via the My Computer icon and then the Control Panel icon we shall create a *shortcut*.

4 DRAG the **Date/Time** icon out of the window and place it on the desktop.

A Warning window appears telling you that you cannot do this:

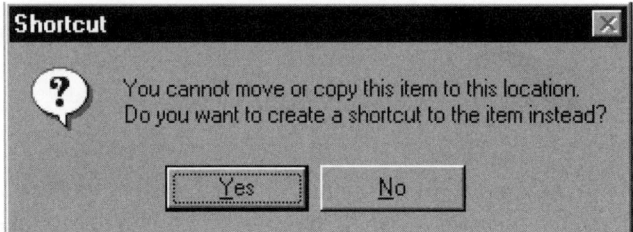

You can, however, create a shortcut to the facility offered by this icon as is stated in the Warning window.

5 CLICK the **Yes** button and an icon similar to the Date/Time icon appears on the desktop.

Notice that the Date/Time icon is still residing in the Control Panel window.

6 CLOSE the **Control Panel** window and then close the My Computer window.

The desktop is now in its original state except for the Shortcut to Date/Time icon.

7 DOUBLE-CLICK the **Shortcut to Date-Time** icon to reveal the Date/Time Properties window.

Using this shortcut facility we can employ the desktop as a storage area for icons where each icon provides a simple and quick access point to frequently used facilities.

8 CLOSE the Date/Time Properties window.

Activity 4.3   Tidying up the desktop

Just like an ordinary desk with papers and books everywhere we need, every now and then, to tidy up a desktop cluttered with icons.

1   ENSURE that the desktop is on display.

2   DRAG each icon to another position on the desktop in a random fashion until you have a messy layout.

3   POINT at a clear area of the desktop and CLICK the **right-hand** mouse button.

A small window appears containing a collection of options:

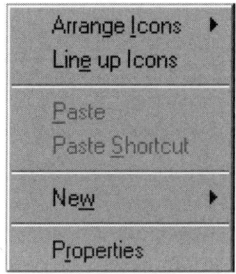

4   SELECT **Line up Icons**

All the icons line up as though there were a grid of horizontal and vertical lines on the screen and where each icon has snapped into position to the nearest intersection of a pair of horizontal and vertical lines.

5   CLICK the right-hand mouse button again but this time SELECT **Arrange Icon**s. This time a second menu of options appears:

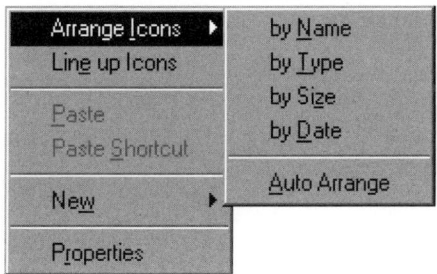

6   SELECT any one of by Name, Type, Size or Date and the icons immediately range themselves down the left hand side of the desktop. That's a lot tidier.

7   MOVE the icons again to random positions on the screen, click the right-hand mouse button, select Arrange Icons and then select Auto Arrange.

8   Try to DRAG an icon away from its position and when you release the mouse button it snaps back to where it was. Auto Arrange is on. If you were to drag the icon and place it on top of another icon then they would change places.

9   CLICK the right-hand mouse button again, SELECT **Arrange Icons** and you will see that there is a tick against Auto Arrange to indicate that this facility is switched on.

10 SELECT Auto Arrange again and this turns the facility off as you will see when you drag an icon across the desktop again.

| Task 5 | # The Recycle bin

> **Deleting unwanted files**

Many times you may find the desktop becomes cluttered with icons that you no longer want and, fortunately, there is a simple method of disposing of them.

Ensure that the desktop is on display.

Activity 5.1 Disposing of an unwanted shortcut file

1 OPEN the **My Computer** window, followed by the Control Panel window and CREATE another shortcut icon for the Date/Time.

You will see that this icon is identical to the first shortcut icon except for the number 2 indicating that it is a duplicate.

2 DRAG this second **Date/Time** icon until it is over the Recycle bin and RELEASE the mouse button. This process is known as *drag and drop*.

The icon then falls into the bin. That has removed it from the desktop. Now to remove it from the bin.

3 DOUBLE-CLICK the **Recycle bin** icon to reveal the Recycle Bin window:

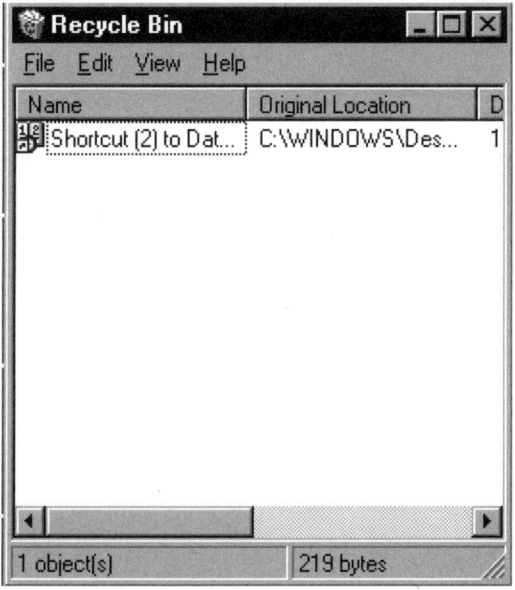

This window contains an information panel that contains a small graphic and description indicating that the duplicate shortcut icon is in there.

4   CLICK the **File** command on the Menu bar of the Recycle Bin window to reveal a drop-down list of further options:

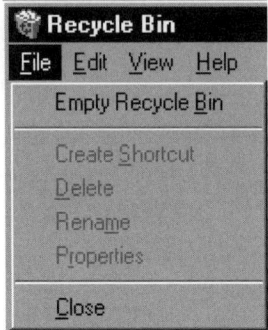

5   SELECT **Empty Recycle Bin** and respond to the question that appears in the Confirm File Delete window by clicking the **Yes** button.

The graphic in the window's information panel disappears indicating that it has been disposed of.

6   CLOSE the **Recycle bin** window.

The duplicate icon has now been erased forever.

| Task 6 | # The Task bar |

➤ Using the Task bar

At the bottom of the screen is the Task bar and it is here where a record of open windows is stored.

Ensure that the desktop is on display.

Activity 6.1   **The Taskbar Properties window**

1 CLICK the **Start** button and SELECT the **Settings** option to reveal a further menu of options:

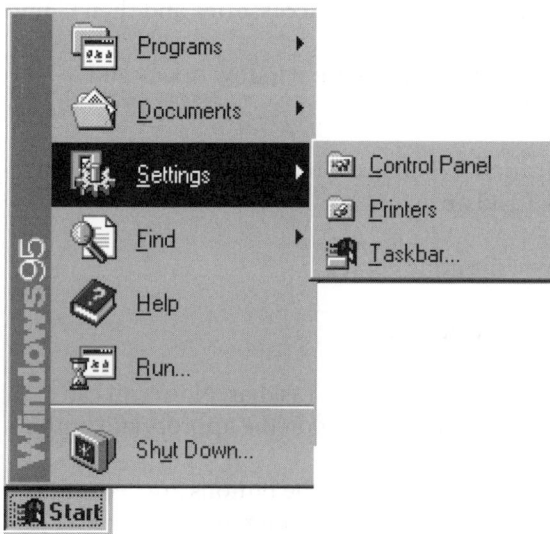

2 SELECT the **Taskbar** option to reveal the Taskbar Properties window which contains two tabbed dialog boxes, one behind the other, whose tabs are labelled Taskbar Options and Start Menu Programs.

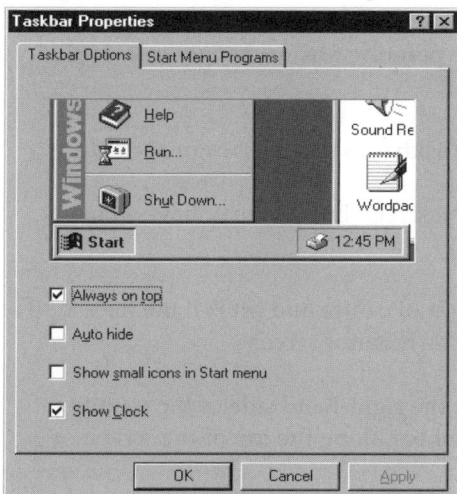

3 CLICK each of the check boxes in the Taskbar Options dialog box in turn to see the effect they have.

4 CLICK the **Start Menu Options** tab and bring that dialog box to the front.

5 COMPLETE this activity with the Taskbar set to be always on top and showing the clock and the Taskbar Properties window closed.

Activity 6.2   The Taskbar as a store of icons

1 ENSURE that the desktop is on display

2 CLICK the **Start** button, SELECT **Programs** followed by **Accessories** and then **Games**.

3 SELECT **Solitaire** from the Games menu and the Solitaire window opens and a Solitaire button appears on the Taskbar.

4 REPEAT this procedure and open up another Solitaire window and you will see a second Solitaire button appear on the Taskbar.

For some applications it is possible to open multiple copies.

5 OPEN up as many **Accessories** options as you wish.

Each time you open an option a new button appears on the Taskbar. Now you can instantly switch from one application to another by clicking on the appropriate buttons on the Taskbar.
   If you have opened up so many Accessories options that the buttons are becoming unrecognizable it is possible to stretch the Taskbar to make more room.

Activity 6.3   Manipulating the Taskbar

1 POINT at the top edge of the Taskbar and the pointing arrow changes to a double-headed arrow.

2 PRESS the mouse button and STRETCH the Taskbar to twice its original depth.

You may not like the Taskbar at the bottom of the screen but you may have so many icons on it that you need to display it.

3 POINT in the middle of the Taskbar to the right of centre and MOVE the mouse so as to drag the task bar to the right-hand side of the monitor screen.

The Task bar moves to a vertical position down the right-hand side of the monitor screen. In a similar way you can re-locate the Taskbar along the top of the screen or down the left-hand side. Try it.

Section A   Summary

You may be starting to feel a little overwhelmed by all that you have done so far. This is quite understandable, especially if you have never handled a system like this before. It seems that there is so much to remember and so many things to do. If this is how you are reacting then take a breather and come back to it later. Meanwhile, just stop and think about why this system was designed in the first place. It was designed the way it was to make operating a computer simpler than hitherto. Simpler! you might exclaim. If this is simple ..! The point about the graphical user interface is that it *is* simple. However, it only becomes so with use and experience. The one thing you do not have to do is to remember long lists of esoteric commands for performing tasks that you did not even know could be performed.

Section B

The Start button options

By now you should have a good idea of what windows are, how they can be moved, re-sized, opened and closed. You have seen icons and you now should appreciate that an icon is a gateway to an application – some facility that enables you to do something. A little vague I agree but in this next section we shall see just what you can do with various available applications.

By accessing the various features that Windows 95 has to offer via the Start button you will learn how to:

- navigate your way around the system
- use the wordprocessing facilities offered by WordPad
- create pictures in Paint
- place a Paint image inside a WordPad document
- link WordPad and Paint together using an Object

In addition, you will gain further experience of manipulating the graphical user interface and begin to develop an appreciation of the 'feel' of Windows 95.

Task 7:   Accessories
Task 8:   The WordPad accessory
Task 9:   Creating a document in WordPad
Task 10: Printing a document
Task 11: Starting to use the Paint accessory
Task 12: The Paint accessory in detail
Task 13: Drawing a diagram
Task 14: Using Paint to enhance a WordPad document
Task 15: Placing an Object into a document

| Task 7 | # Accessories

> ➤ **The various accessories that are available within Windows 95**

Ensure that the desktop is on display

Activity 7.1 **Accessing Accessories**

1 CLICK the **Start** button, SELECT Programs form the Start menu and Accessories from the Programs menu.

A list of Accessories is displayed:

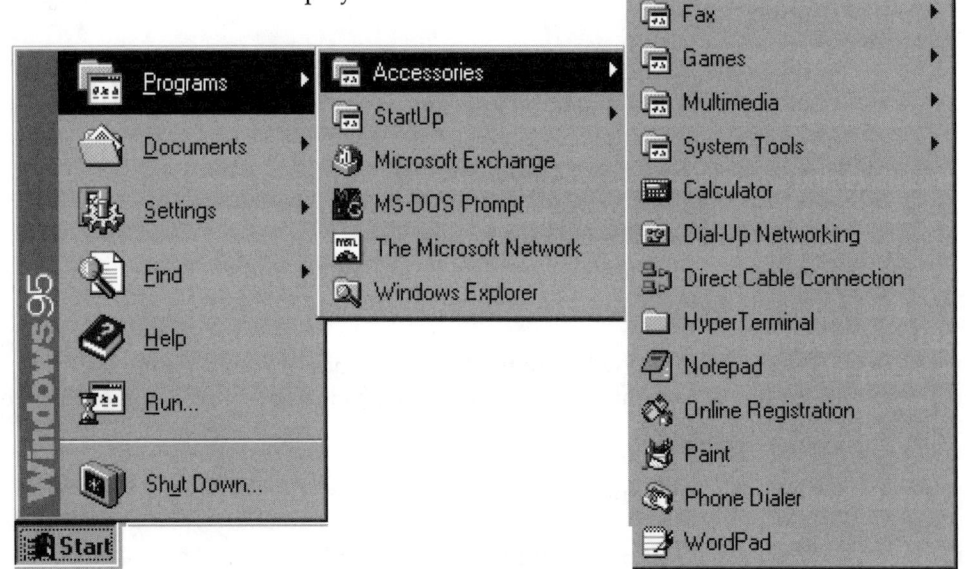

2 SELECT the last accessory on the list, **WordPad** to reveal the WordPad window:

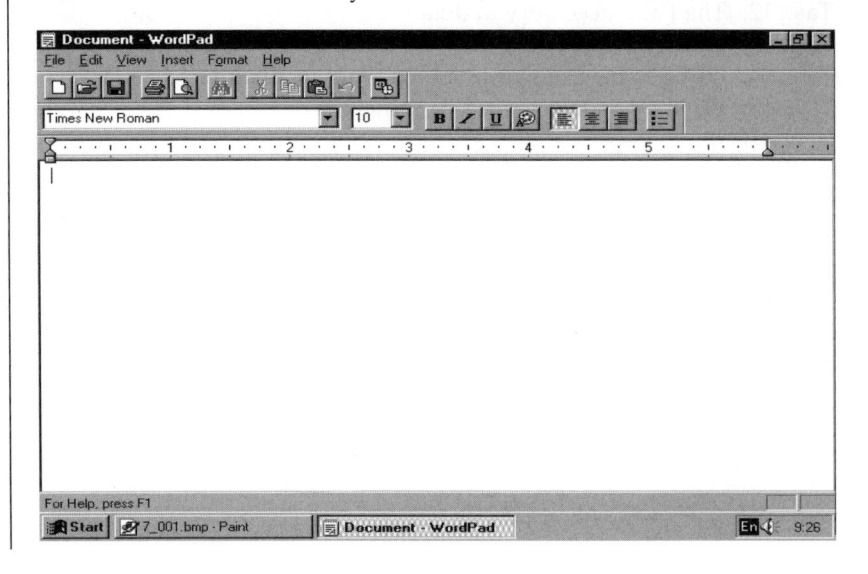

26 The Start button options

WordPad is a wordprocessor with many of the features that you would find in a stand-alone word processor package such as Microsoft's Word 6. We shall look at how to create a document in the next Task. For now, let us look at some other Accessories.

3   OPEN the **Paint** accessory window via the Start button and the Programs selection.

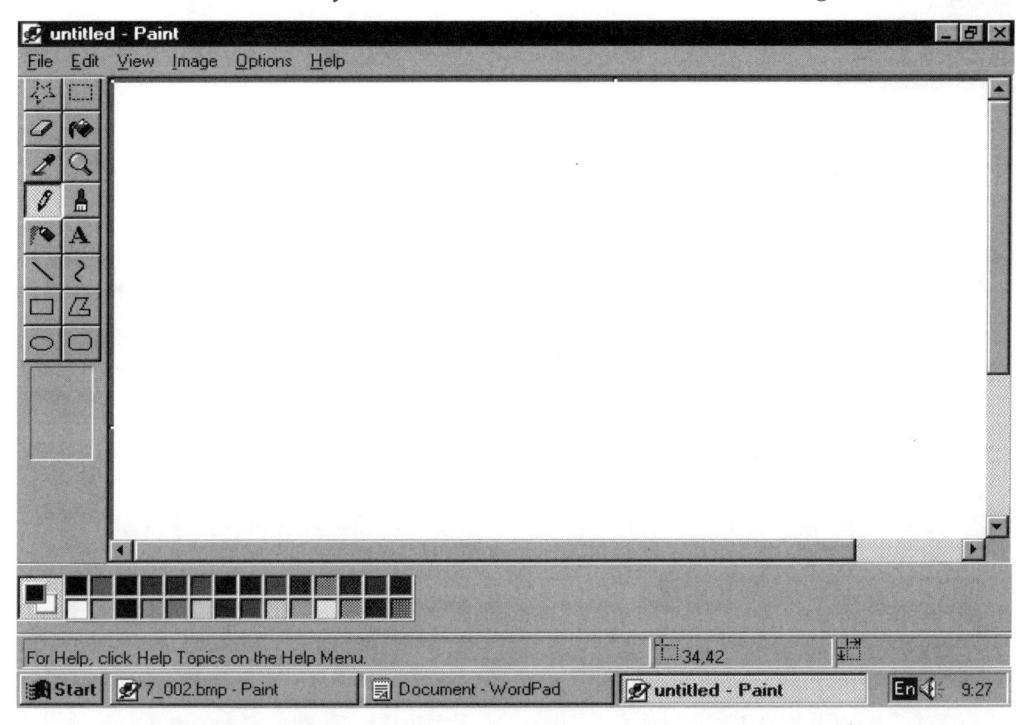

Paint is an application that enables you to construct pictures. Down the left-hand side of the window are all the tools that are available such as brush, aerosol and eraser and ranged across the bottom of the window are all the colours that are available. Pictures created in Paint can be very easily copied into a document created in WordPad and we shall see how to do this in Task 14.

4   OPEN the **Calculator** accessory window via the Start button, the Programs and the Accessories selection.

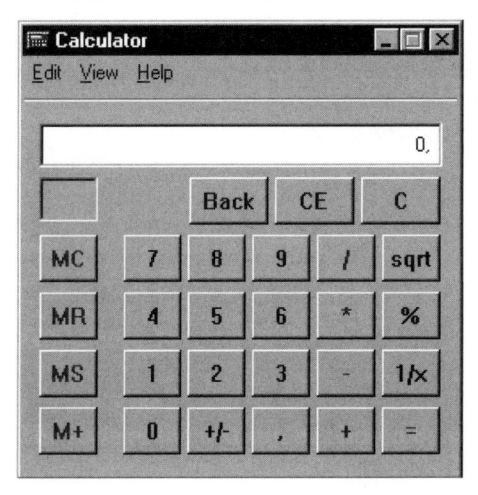

The on-line calculator comes in two guises, standard and scientific.

5 CLICK the **View** command on the Calculator window and a drop-down menu appears:

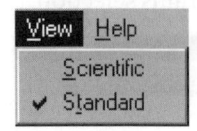

```
View  Help
   Scientific
 ✓ Standard
```

6 SELECT **Standard** and **Scientific** alternately to see the difference between the two calculators:

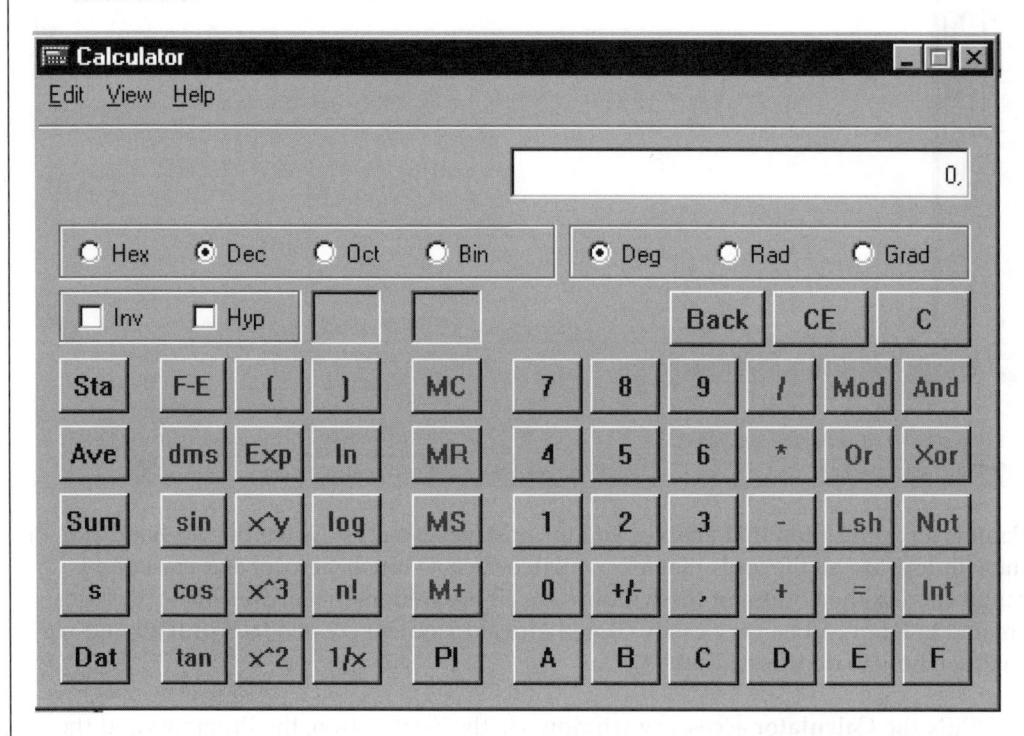

By now you will have three applications open and three corresponding buttons on the Task bar.

28 The Start button options

| Task 8 | # The WordPad accessory

➤ **Manipulating text within WordPad**

Ensure that the desktop is on display

Activity 8.1   Entering text into Wordpad

1   Either CLICK the **WordPad** button on the Task bar to reveal the WordPad window or, if the WordPad button is not on the Task bar, OPEN the **WordPad** window via the Start button.

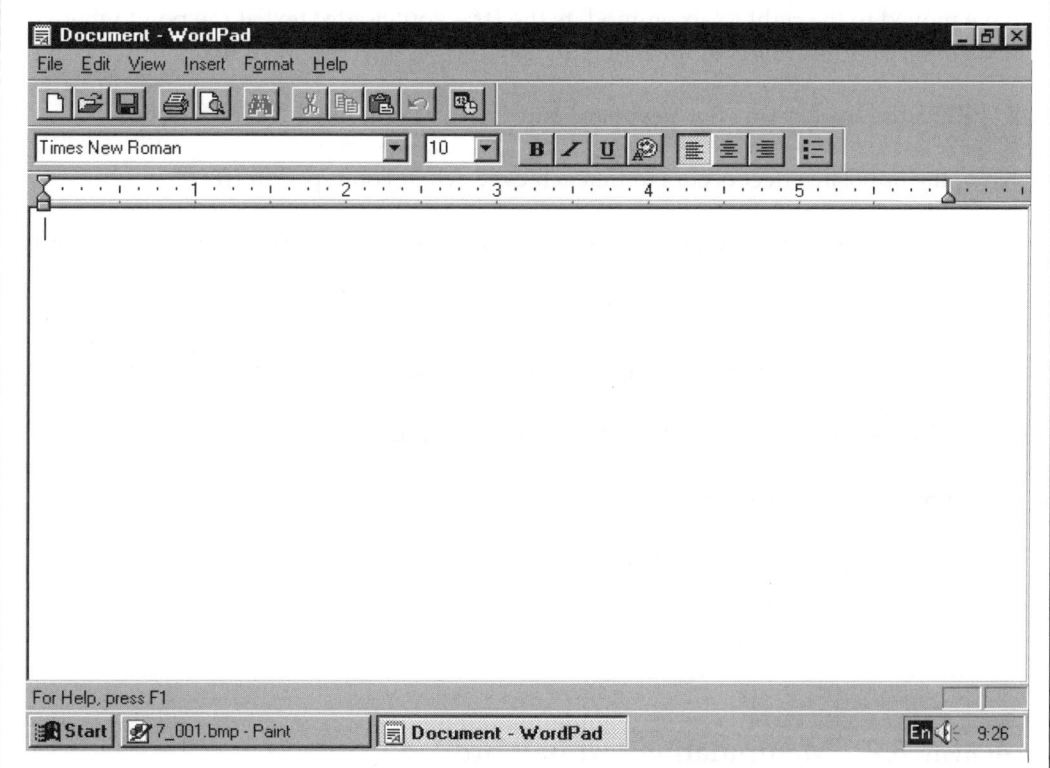

The text cursor – a vertical line – is flashing in the top left hand corner of the document area. This is tell you that if you were to type text at the keyboard this is where is would appear on the screen. If the text corsor has not appeared just click the body of the WordPad window.

2   TYPE in the following sentence:

The lazy brown fox jumped over the stile

3   MOVE the mouse and you will see that the mouse pointer is now in the form of an elongated I-section

Here we have to distinguish between the pointer, which is the I-section and the text cursor which is the flashing, vertical line in the text. When you type, the keyboard characters appear at the flashing cursor's location. This location can be changed by using the mouse pointer.

4   MOVE the mouse pointer next to, but to the left of, the letter **f** of **fox** and CLICK the mouse button.

Now you see that the text cursor has moved to this spot.

5   TYPE in **fff**.

One of two things will have happened. Either the word **fox** and all the text following it have moved to the right to accommodate the **fff** – you *inserted* text at the point where the text cursor was flashing. Or, the letters **fff** have *overwritten* the word fox.

7   PRESS the **Ins** key on your keyboard and then TYPE in the three letters **ooo**.

Now, the opposite effect occurs to that achieved when you typed in **fff**.

- Text is entered via the keyboard and it appears on the screen where the text cursor is located.
- The text cursor can be re-located using the mouse pointer.
- Text entered in the middle of existing text will either cause the existing text to move to the right – the new text will be inserted into the old text – or it will overwrite the existing text.
- The **Ins** key on the keyboard is a *toggle switch* that turns the Insert mode on and off.

7   PRESS the **Backspace** key.

The text cursor moves to the left and in doing so erases the letter it moves over. All the text to the right is pulled back with the text cursor. This is a simple way to delete characters and words.

Activity 8.2   Manipulating text in WordPad

1   ENSURE that you have the text:

The lazy brown fox jumped over the stile

on display. If necessary change what you do have by inserting text, overwriting text or deleting text until you end up with this sentence.

2   PLACE the mouse pointer to the left of the word brown, HOLD DOWN the left-hand mouse button and then DRAG the pointer to the right of the word. This is called *selecting* the text.

The word brown now becomes highlighted – we say it is highlighted in reverse video because instead of its display being dark letters on a white background its display becomes white letters on a dark background. By highlighting the word brown in this way the word had been *selected*.

The lazy brown fox jumped over the stile

3   PRESS the **Backspace** key and the word brown disappears.

The backspace key will delete any selected text.

4   RE-TYPE the word brown and HIGHLIGHT it again in reverse video.

5   TYPE in the letter **x**.

Again, the word brown disappears only this time is is replaced by the letter x. Any selected text will be replaced by the next keystroke.

6   RE-TYPE in the word **brown**.

7   PLACE the mouse pointer in the middle of the word brown and DOUBLE-CLICK the mouse button.

Again the word brown is selected. Double-clicking a word has the same effect as selecting it with the mouse pointer.

8   CLICK the **Edit** command on the Menu bar to reveal a drop-down menu of further commands:

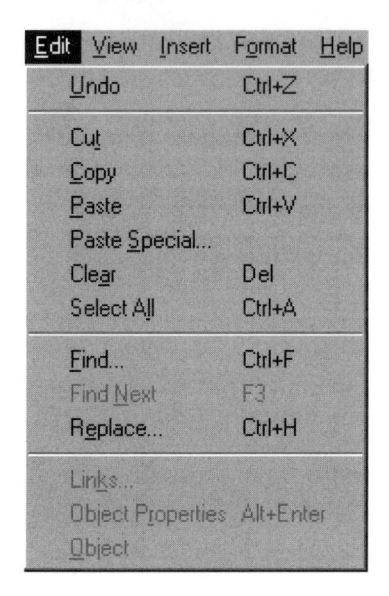

Edit	View	Insert	Format	Help
Undo		Ctrl+Z		
Cut		Ctrl+X		
Copy		Ctrl+C		
Paste		Ctrl+V		
Paste Special...				
Clear		Del		
Select All		Ctrl+A		
Find...		Ctrl+F		
Find Next		F3		
Replace...		Ctrl+H		
Links...				
Object Properties		Alt+Enter		
Object				

9   SELECT the **Copy** command and the drop-down menu closes.

Nothing has appeared to happen.

10 ENSURE that the text cursor is flashing immediately after the word stile (use the mouse pointer to re-locate it if necessary).

11 CLICK the **Edit** command on the Menu bar and this time SELECT the **Paste** option.

The word **brown** has appeared immediately after the word **stile**.

This effect is part of what is known as *Cutting and Pasting*. When you *Copy* a piece of selected text it is copied into a reserved area of the computer's memory. Then when you activate the *Paste* command from the Edit menu you produce a copy at the location of the text cursor of whatever is in the reserved area of memory. In earlier versions of Windows this reserved area of memory is called the Clipboard and it was possible to view the contents of the Clipboard. In Windows 95 the Clipboard is not accessible to viewing though it is still present within the system.

12 SELECT the word **fox**.

13 CLICK the **Edit** command on the Menu bar and SELECT the option **Cut**.

The word fox disappears – it has been cut out.

14 LOCATE the text cursor at the end of the sentence and SELECT **Paste** from the Edit menu.

The word fox appears. When you Cut a selection of text a copy is made and placed on the Clipboard and whatever is on the Clipboard can be Pasted into the document.

Activity 8.3 Enhancing text in Wordpad

1 ENSURE that you have the text:

   The lazy brown fox jumped over the stile

   on display. If necessary, re-type it.

2 SELECT the word **stile**.

3 CLICK the **B** button on the Tool bar.

4 CLICK anywhere in the text to remove the highlight from the word **stile**.

The word stile now appears in emboldened print. The **B** button enhances selected text by emboldening it.

The lazy brown fox jumped over the **stile**

5 SELECT the word **stile** again.

6 CLICK the *I* button on the Tool bar.

7 CLICK anywhere in the text to remove the highlight from the word **stile**.

The emboldened word stile now is also italicized. The *I* button enhances selected text by italicizing it.

*The lazy brown fox jumped over the **stile***

8 SELECT the word **stile** for the third time.

9 CLICK the **U** button on the Tool bar.

10 CLICK anywhere in the text to remove the highlight from the word **stile**.

The italicized and emboldened word stile is now underlined. The **U** button enhances selected text by underlining it.

*The lazy brown fox jumped over the **stile***

Activity 8.4   Manipulating blocks of text in WordPad

The Tool bar contains a number of facilities that can be used to enhance selected text.

1 MOVE the pointer to each button in turn and wait. A small box appears at the side of the button describing the effect that pressing the button will achieve.

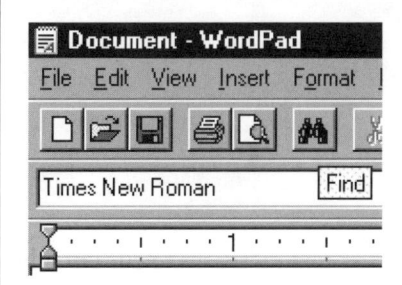

On the left-hand side of the Tool bar you will see the Font list box:

2 ENSURE that the sentence

   The lazy brown fox jumped over the stile

   is on display.

3 POINT at any part of this sentence and *triple-click* the mouse button.

The entire sentence is then selected.

4   CLICK the **down arrow** at the side of the Font list box to reveal a list of available fonts:

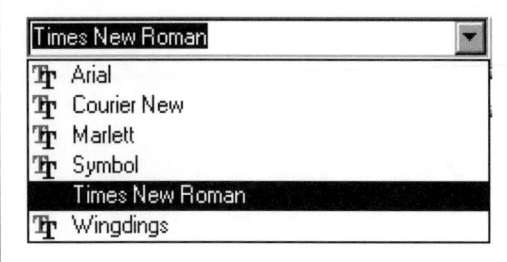

```
Times New Roman        ▼
 Tr  Arial
 Tr  Courier New
 Tr  Marlett
 Tr  Symbol
     Times New Roman
 Tr  Wingdings
```

5   CLICK the font **Arial**.

The Font list box closes and the font of the selected text changes to Arial font. Try other fonts until you are happy that you are clear about what you are doing.
   To the right of the Font box is the Font Size list box.

6   CLICK the **down-arrow** at the side of the Font Size list box to reveal a list of font sizes.

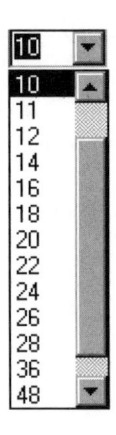

```
10   ▼
10   ▲
11
12
14
16
18
20
22
24
26
28
36
48   ▼
```

7   CLICK the size **20**.

The Font Size list box closes and the font size of the selected text increases to 20. Try other sizes to see the effect but finish with the smallest font size 8.

To the left of the Tool bar are three alignment buttons:

These buttons provide the facility to left, centre or right justify selected text.

8   SELECT the entire sentence and click each of these three buttons in turn to see their effect.

9   CLICK the **Bullets** button and you will see a bullet appear to the left of the sentence

10 CLICK the **Color** button and a list box of colours appears:

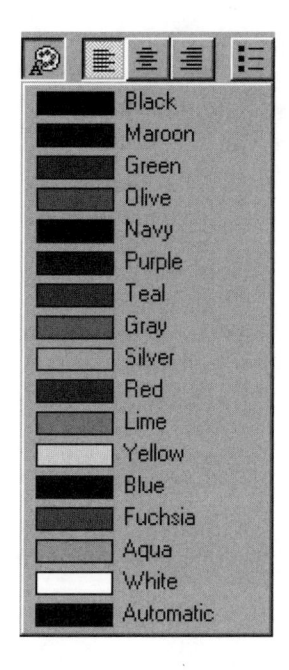

11 SELECT any colour you wish and the list box closes.

12 DE-SELECT the text by clicking anywhere in the document and you will see it written in the colour of your choice.

Activity 8.5 Using the ruler

At the top of the document area, just below the Tool bar you will see the Ruler:

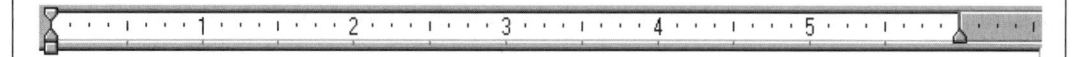

The Ruler is used to set the width of the print on the page, to set the paragraph indents and to set the tabs. The default Ruler extends across six inches from 0 (not marked on the Ruler) to 6.

1 ENSURE that the sentence:

   The lazy brown fox jumped over the stile

   is on display in Times New Roman font, point size 10. Also, make sure that there is a single space after the word stile.

2 COPY this entire sentence, PLACE the text cursor at the end of the sentence and then PASTE in six copies of the sentence after which you will have a paragraph of text about three lines long.

3 SELECT the entire paragraph of text and DRAG the right-hand end triangular Ruler marker back to the number 5 on the Ruler.

The effect on the text is to reduce its maximum width from 6 inches to 5 inches.

4 With the entire paragraph still selected DRAG the top left-hand triangular Ruler marker to the number 1 on the Ruler.

The effect is to indent the first line of the paragraph by 1 inch.

5 DRAG the top left-hand marker back to 0 and then DRAG the bottom left-hand triangular marker to the number 1 on the Ruler.

This has the reverse effect in that the first line of the paragraph is not indented but the rest of the paragraph is.

6 DRAG the bottom left-hand triangular Ruler marker back to 0 and then DRAG the bottom left-hand square marker to the number 1 on the Ruler.

This has a similar effect to moving the right-hand marker in that it reduces the maximum width of the selected text.

7 DRAG the bottom left-hand square marker back to 0 on the Ruler.

8 CLICK the number 1 on the Ruler and a bold **L** appears. REPEAT this to place a bold **L** on the number 2.

The bold **L** is the position of a tab stop marker.

9 PLACE the text cursor to the immediate left of the first line of the text and PRESS the **Tab** key on the keyboard.

The text is then tabbed to the first tab stop marker.

10 REPEAT this and you will see the text tabbed to the second tab stop marker.

11 REPEAT again and this time you will see the text tabbed to the $2^{1}/_{2}$ inches position even though there is no tab stop marker there.

There are default tab stops every half inch along the Ruler but they are not marked. These default tab stop markers can be over-ridden by clicking the Ruler and placing a tab stop marker where you wish it to be.

12 DRAG and DROP the first tab stop marker off the Ruler and the tab stop marker disappears.

Marked tab stops can be removed simply by dragging them off the Ruler.

Task 9   # Creating a document in WordPad

➤ **Creating a well constructed and formatted document complete with enhancements**

Ensure that WordPad is on display.

Activity 9.1   **Entering the text**

In this Activity we are going to enter text into a WordPad document. In the next Activity we shall edit the document so there is no need to be concerned in this Activity with the way that the document looks. You will need to take care about spelling though because there is no spellchecker in WordPad.

First we need to clear away any text that is currently on the screen.

1   PLACE the mouse pointer at the top left-hand corner of the document area, HOLD DOWN the **shift** key, place the cursor at the end of the text and CLICK so as to select the text.

2   PRESS the **backspace** key to clear all the selected text.

Now the document area is clear and ready to accept text but before we do this, a word of caution. When you type text into a document the text actually resides in the computer's memory. If a power failure caused your computer to turn off then all that text in memory would be lost. To avoid losses like this we save the document to disk at periodic intervals.

3   CLICK the **File** command on the Menu bar to reveal a drop-down menu of further options:

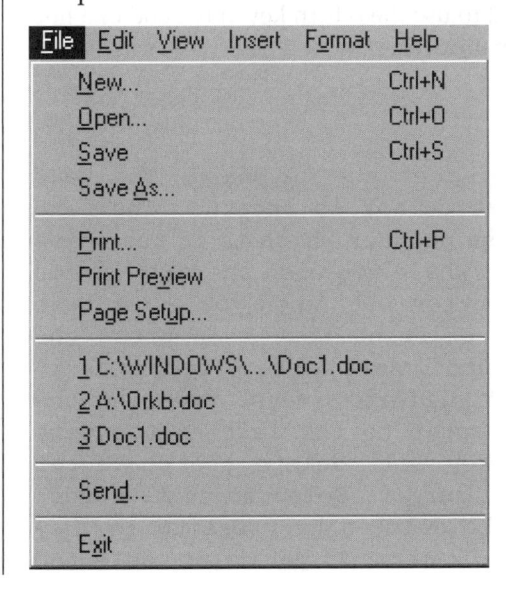

```
File   Edit   View   Insert   Format   Help
  New...                        Ctrl+N
  Open...                       Ctrl+O
  Save                          Ctrl+S
  Save As...

  Print...                      Ctrl+P
  Print Preview
  Page Setup...

  1 C:\WINDOWS\...\Doc1.doc
  2 A:\Orkb.doc
  3 Doc1.doc

  Send...

  Exit
```

4 SELECT the **Save As...** option to reveal the Save As dialog box:

```
Save As                                                    ? X
Save in:    [Desktop]              ▼  [icons]
    My Computer
    Network Neighborhood
    My Briefcase




File name:    [Document.doc]                    [  Save  ]
Save as type: [Word for Windows 6.0]        ▼   [ Cancel ]
```

5 In the **File name** box TYPE in the name:

   Doc1

Notice the **Save in** box contains the location Desktop – the document will be saved and left on the desktop.

6 CLICK the **Save** button and the document is saved to the hard disk but its icon remains on the desktop.

Now we are ready to enter the text.

7 TYPE in the following text (you do not need to use the return key at the end of a line, the text wraps round to the next line automatically):

```
Document Editing
Adding, deleting and moving text
Adding text. Text is added by typing at the keyboard. The text
appears at the place where the text cursor is located. The text
cursor can be moved by using the mouse pointer which is in the shape
of an I section. Place the pointer to where you wish the text cursor
to be located and click the mouse button. If, when you enter text
at the keyboard it overwrites the existing text then press the
Ins(ert) key to put the text entry into insert mode. Deleting text.
Text can be deleted in a number of different ways. Pressing the
backspace key will delete the character to the left of the text
cursor and pressing the Del(ete) key will delete the character
immediately to the right of the text cursor. Selected text, words,
sentences or whole paragraphs can be deleted by pressing any key
or by using the Cut command from the Edit menu. If you delete selected
```

```
text by using any key then the character that corresponds to that
key will appear in place of the deleted text. Moving text. Selected
text can be moved by using the Cut and Paste options from the Edit
menu or simply by pointing to the selected text and dragging it to
the desired location. Enhancing text. Type style. The style of the
text can be chosen by using any one of the B(old), I(talic),
U(nderline) or Color buttons on the Tool bar. Type font and size.
There is a number of different fonts available from the Font list
box and a range of sizes available from the Font Size list box.
```

8. When the document is complete CLICK the **File** command on the Menu bar and SELECT the **Save** option.

Because you have previously given this file a name and designated that it lie on the desktop the file is automatically saved to disk updating the earlier copy.

Activity 9.2   Editing the document

1. USE all the editing and enhancement tools that we have described so far to produce a document that looks like the following:

Document Editing

Adding, Deleting and Moving Text

- *Adding Text*

Text is added by typing at the keyboard. The text appears at the place where the text cursor is located. The text cursor can be moved by using the mouse pointer which is in the shape of an I section. Place the pointer to where you wish the text cursor to be located and click the mouse button. If, when you enter text at the keyboard it overwrites the existing text then press the **Ins**(ert) key to put the text entry into insert mode.

- *Deleting Text*

Text can be deleted in a number of different ways. Pressing the **Backspace** key will delete the character to the left of the text cursor and pressing the **Del**(ete) key will delete the character immediately to the right of the text cursor. Selected text, words, sentences or whole paragraphs can be deleted by pressing any key or by using the **Cut** command from the **Edit** menu. If you delete selected text by using any key then the character that corresponds to that key will appear in place of the deleted text.

- *Moving Text*

Selected text can be moved by using the **Cut** and **Paste** options from the **Edit** menu or simply by pointing to the selected text and dragging it to the desired location.

Enhancing Text

- *Type Style*

The style of the text can be chosen by using any one of the **B**(old), **I**(talic), **U**(nderline) or **Color** buttons on the Tool bar.

- *Type Font and Size*

Different fonts are available from the **Font** list box and a range of sizes is available from the **Font Size** list box.

2 When the editing is complete SAVE the document to disk.

3 CLICK the WordPad **Close** button and close the application.

The document has been saved to disk in its final form and the means whereby it has been produced has been closed. The document, however, resides on the desktop as can be seen from its icon:

Doc1.doc

Notice that the name of the document is Doc1.doc. The extension .doc has been added automatically by WordPad bcause that is how WordPad recognizes files.

| Task 10 | Printing a document |

➤ **Sending a document to the printer**

Ensure that the desktop is on display

Activity 10.1 Printing the document

Having produced a document in WordPad that has the appearance that you require the time has come to produce a hard copy – to produce a printed version.

1. DOUBLE-CLICK the **Doc1.doc** icon on the desktop.

This causes the WordPad application to be brought into memory with the Doc1 document on display.

2. CLICK the **File** command and from the File menu SELECT the **Print** option to reveal the Print dialog box:

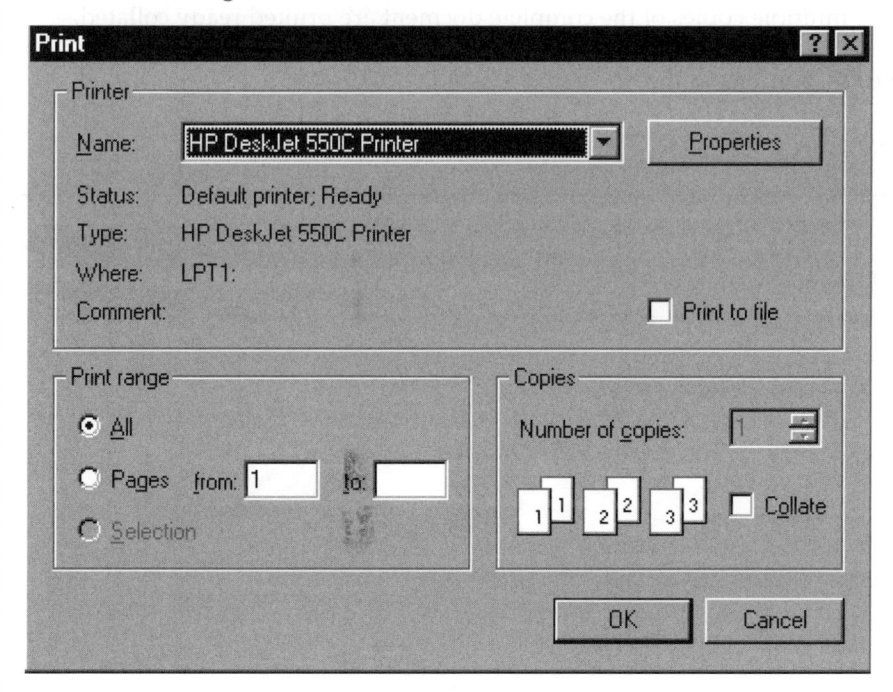

```
Print                                                          ? X
┌─Printer─────────────────────────────────────────────────────┐
│ Name:    [HP DeskJet 550C Printer        ▼]  [Properties]   │
│ Status:  Default printer; Ready                             │
│ Type:    HP DeskJet 550C Printer                            │
│ Where:   LPT1:                                              │
│ Comment:                                    ☐ Print to file │
└─────────────────────────────────────────────────────────────┘
┌─Print range──────────────┐  ┌─Copies──────────────────────┐
│ ⦿ All                    │  │ Number of copies:  [1] ⇅    │
│ ○ Pages  from: [1] to:[ ]│  │  [1][2][3]    ☐ Collate     │
│ ○ Selection              │  │                             │
└──────────────────────────┘  └─────────────────────────────┘
                                         [  OK  ]  [ Cancel ]
```

3. ENSURE that the settings in the Print dialog box are:

Printer
This should display the name of the printer you are going to use. If it displays another printer's name then CLICK the **down arrow** at the end of the list box and SELECT the printer you wish to use from the list of options displayed.

Printing a document 41

Print range
SELECT the radio button **All**.
Notice that it is also possible to print specific pages.

Copies
SELECT Number of copies to be **1**.

Notice the Collate check box. If you wanted to print multiple copies of a document but you had not chosen to collate them then multiple copies of each page would be printed together. If you elect to collate by clicking the Collate check box the graphic display changes:

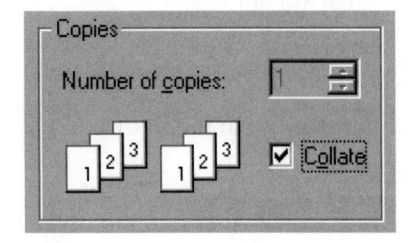

In this case the multiple copies of the complete docment are printed ready collated.

4   CLICK the **OK** button and the document is sent to the printer.

5   When the pinting is complete CLOSE DOWN the WordPad application.

| Task 11 | Starting to use the Paint accessory

> **Accessing and using the various features offered in the Paint accessory**

Ensure that the desktop is on display.

Activity 11.1 Accessing Paint

1 From the Accessories list via the Start button and the Programs selection, SELECT the accessory Paint to reveal the Paint window:

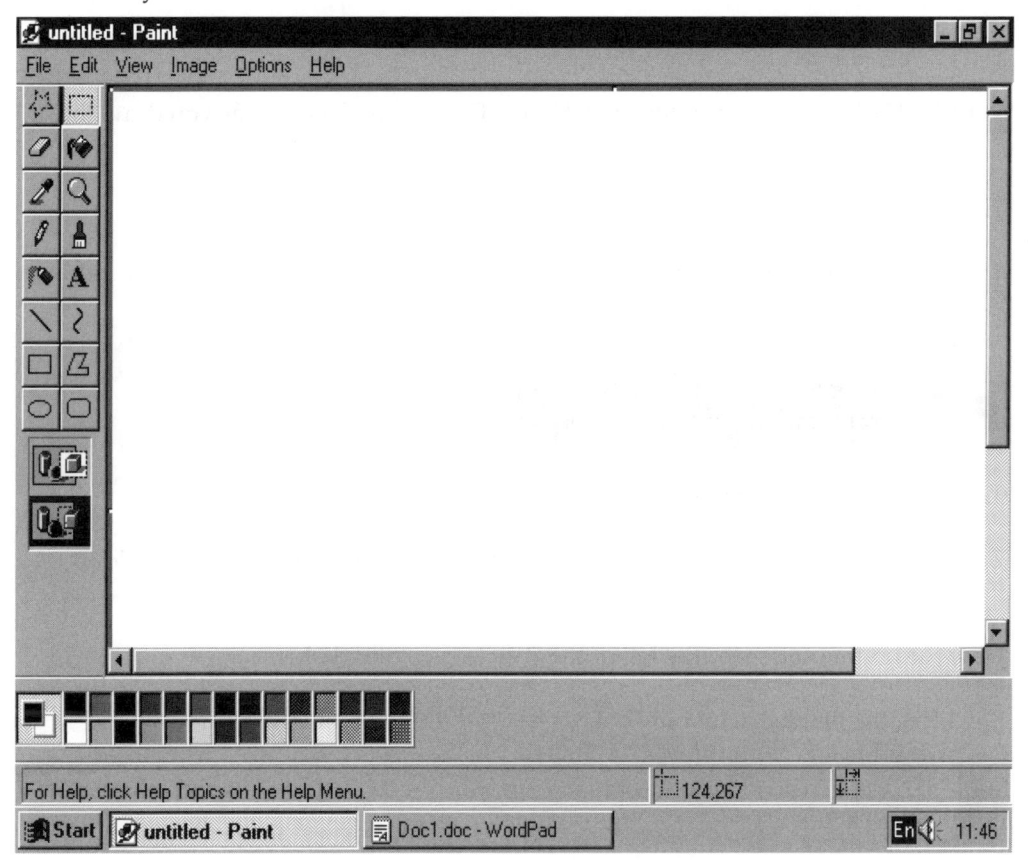

Using Paint you can create all manner of pictures ranging from formal diagrams containing regular shapes such as rectangles, lines and circles to freehand drawings of whatever takes your fancy. The screen that you see before you has a clear central area – the drawing area – in which you can indulge your artistic endeavours by using drawing tools that are arrayed in the Tool bar down the left-hand side of the screen. Along the bottom of the screen is your colour palette and along the top of the drawing area is the Menu bar that contains a selection of commands similar to those that you met in WordPad.

The Tool Bar contains a collection of sixteen tools, each accessed by clicking the appropriate button. We shall consider each button in detail later. For now we will just play a little.

2   CLICK the **Rectangle** button which is the seventh button down on the extreme left of the Tool bar:

3   MOVE the mouse pointer into the drawing area where you will see that it has changed and is now in the form of a cross.

4   DEPRESS the left-hand mouse button and MOVE the mouse over the worktop.

A rectangle appears in the drawing area.

5   REPEAT this process but this time, HOLD DOWN the Shift key as you draw the rectangle.

This time the rectangle is a square.

6   CLICK the bright green square on the Colour Palette at the bottom of the window.

To the extreme left of the Colour Palette are two squares, one inside the other:

The top square is now coloured green.

7   Using the right-hand mouse button CLICK the dark blue square on the Colour Palette.

Now the bottom square to the left of the Palette is coloured blue.

8   CLICK the **Paint Can** on the Tool bar (second down on the right):

9   MOVE the mouse pointer (now in the shape of a paint can) until the pointer is inside the rectangle drawn earlier and then CLICK the left-hand mouse button.

The interior of the rectangle fills with green.

10 MOVE the mouse pointer to the interior of the square and then CLICK the right-hand mouse button.

The square fills with the colour blue. This is how the Colour Palette works. The two selected colours apply to the left- and right-hand mouse buttons respectively.

11 CLICK the **Rectangle** button again.

At the bottom of the Tool bar is a panel:

This panel offers optional rectangles.

12 CLICK the shaded rectangle with a boundary – the second one down.

13 Now DRAW a rectangle with the left-hand mouse button depressed.

The rectangle is drawn with a green boundary and a blue interior.

14 DRAW a rectangle with the right-hand mouse button depressed.

The opposite effect – a blue rectangle with a green interior.

15 With the right-hand mouse button SELECT **white** on the colour palette.

16 CLICK the top right-hand button on the Tool Bar – the **Select** button.

17 PLACE the mouse pointer (a cross) just outside the top left-hand corner of the first rectangle that you drew.

18 DEPRESS the left-hand mouse button and MOVE the mouse across the workshop.

A rectangle with a dashed-line boundary appears.

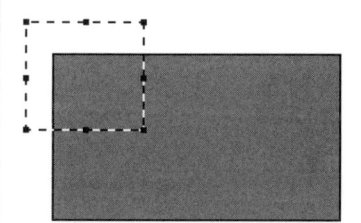

19 ENSURE that the rectangle with the dashed-line boundary contains the top left-hand corner of the rectangle that you originally drew and RELEASE the mouse button.

The rectangle with the dashed-line boundary remains – this indicates the section of the drawing area that has been *selected*.

20 CLICK the **Edit** command on the Menu bar and SELECT the **Cut** option from the drop-down Edit menu.

That section of the rectangle that was contained within the selected area disappears.

21 CLICK the **Edit** menu command and then select the **Paste** option.

The cut section of the rectangle then appears in the top left-hand corner of the drawing area, surrounded by a dashed line rectangle – this pasted section is now selected.

22 PLACE the mouse pointer inside the dashed-line rectangle and you will see it change to a different style of cross.

22 DRAG the selected portion of drawing across the drawing area.

Cutting, Copying and pasting follows exactly the same pattern as it did in WordPad. Anything that is selected using the Select tool can be Copied or Cut via the Edit command. A copy is then placed on the clipboard. The Paste command can then be used to copy the contents of the clipboard into the drawing.

24 CLICK the **File** command and from the File drop-down menu select **Save As...** and save the drawing to the desktop with the name Draw1.

Note: If you had not changed the right-hand mouse button colour from blue to white the selected area would have been blue.

| Task 12 | The Paint accessory in detail

➤ **The facilities offered by the Paint accessory**

Ensure that the Paint window is on display

Activity 12.1 **The Tool Bar**

The Tool Bar contains sixteen buttons:

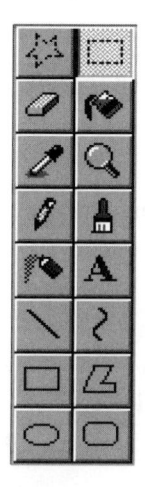

Fre-Form Select and Select
The Free-Form Select has the same effect as the Select button except that you must draw the area to be selected free-hand.

Easer and Fill
The Eraser needs a little care to understand how it works.

1 ENSURE that the drawing from the previous Activity is on display with the green and blue colours selected.

The drawing was saved to the desktop in the previous Activity so double-clicking its icon will retrieve it.

2 CLICK the **Eraser** button and DEPRESS the left-hand mouse button.

3 MOVE the mouse over your worktop and you will see a thick blue line drawn in the drawing area. This blue line will cover whatever it happens to meet.

4 Now DEPRESS the right-hand mouse button and MOVE the eraser across the screen.

This time nothing appears until the eraser meets a green area when it draws a thick blue line over the green.

The Paint Accessory in detail 47

5   CLICK the white square in the colour palette with the right-hand mouse button and repeat the last two instructions.

Now the eraser really does erase when you use the left-hand mouse button – it is in fact drawing a thick white line.

Pick Colour

This button presents a shortcut method of selecting a colour that you have already used.

6   SELECT the colour bright red from the Colour Box to be the active colour for the left-hand mouse button.

7   CLICK the **Pick Colour** button, point at a green area of the screen and click the left-hand mouse button.

You will see from the bottom left-hand end of the Colour Box that the active colour has changed from red to green – green was *picked* from amongst those colours already used.

Magnifier

This tool enables very fine detail to be added to a drawing. The screen that you are looking at consists of a regular array of rows and columns of bright dots called pixels. Using the Magnifier it is possible to draw at the pixel level.

8   CLICK the **Magnifier** and look at the panel below the Tool Bar where you will see that you can magnify up to eight times (8x):

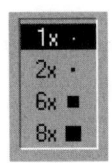

```
1x  ·
2x  ·
6x  ■
8x  ■
```

9   CLICK the **6x** and immediately the screen changes (you may have to use the slider bars to bring the picture into view).

What has happened is that you are now looking at a portion of the screen that has been magnified six times (6x).

10 CLICK the **Pencil** button on the Tool Bar (immediately below the Pick Colour button) and move the cursor to the drawing area.

11 CLICK the drawing area and you will see a small rectangle of solid colour appear.

This is a pixel magnified six times and by using the Pencil tool in this manner you can draw elements of the picture at the pixel level. Notice also the pair of numbers in the small panel on the Status bar:

`17,27`

These give the exact location in the drawing of the point of the pencil – the entire drawing is 640 x 480 pixels in extent where 0,0 refers to the top left-hand corner and 639, 479 refers to the bottom right-hand corner. Other tools can also be used at this level. Try the Paint Can and the Eraser.

Because of the magnification it is not possible to view the entire drawing, but only a section of it. To view other parts of the complete drawing we must make use of the Slider Bars at the right-hand side of and below the drawing area:

12 CLICK the arrows at the ends of the slider bar and you will see the drawing scroll up and down if you are using the vertical slider bar and left and right if you are using the horizontal slider bar.

13 CLICK the space between the end arrows and the slider bar and you will see the drawing scroll up and down a screen depth at a time.

14 DRAG the slider and you will see the drawing move in the appropriate direction.

15 CLICK the **Magnifier** and SELECT **1x** to return to normal size.

Pencil and Brush

From the small panel you can see that the Brush has 12 different possibilites of brush stroke. Try each one of them in turn

Airbrush and Text

The Airbrush gives the effect of a spray can and there are three different densities of spray available.

16 CLICK the **Text** button and then CLICK the drawing area.

A small box opens with a flashing cursor inside. This is where the text will appear when entered at the keyboard. The box is quite small but it will expand to fit the text that is required. Notice that there are two styles of text entered. The first is text with a back ground colour that overlays the drawing (use the right-hand mouse button when locating the cursor in the drawing area) and the second is text without a background colour that merges in with the drawing. Try each in turn.

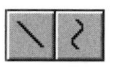

Line and Curve

The Line tools permits straight lines to be drawn. If the Shift key is used simultaneously then the straight lines are restricted to being horizontal, vertical or inclined at 45°. The Curve tool requires a little practice to master its effect.

17 CLICK the **Curve** button on the Tool bar and then try to draw a curve in the drawing area.

18 RELEASE the mouse button.

A straight line appears.

19 PRESS and HOLD DOWN the left-hand mouse button and DRAG the mouse across the worktop.

The effect in the drawing area is to deform the straight line into a curve.

20 RELEASE the mouse button and repeat from another location in the drawing area.

You will see that you get two bites at the cherry. The line is drawn and the you have two chances to deform the line into the desired curve. A deal of practice is required before you can use this tool efficiently.

Rectangle and Polygon

A Polygon is any closed, straight sided figure.

21 SELECT the **Polygon** tool and then draw a line anywhere in the drawing area.

22 MOVE the mouse, CLICK and you will see a line drawn from the point where the first line ended to the end of the mouse pointer.

23 MOVE the mouse again, CLICK and the second line is drawn.

This will continue until you either click on the beginning of the very first line of the polygon or you double-click, in which case a line will appear and close the polygon.

Ellipse and Rounded Rectangle

As with the other geometric shapes, using the Shift key the Ellipse tool will draw a circle and the Rounded Rectangle will draw a square with rounded corners.

24 CLOSE the **Paint** accessory.

| Task 13 | # Drawing a diagram

➤ **Creating a specific diagram**

Activity 13.1 Creating the Paint file

1 ENSURE that the **Paint** accessory is on display, the drawing area is empty and the selected colours are black on white.

This can be achieved either by erasing anything that is drawn or by selecting the **New** option from the **File** command drop-down menu.

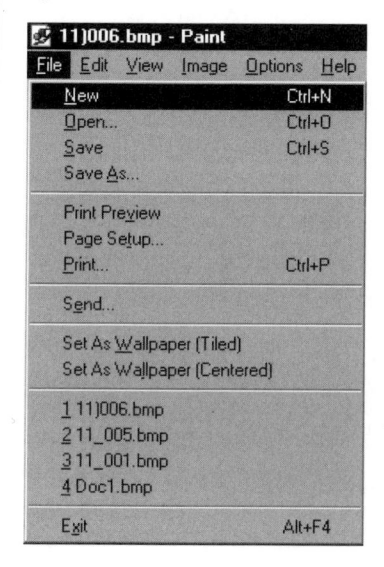

As we did with the WordPad document we shall save this blank drawing area to disk before we start to create the picture

2 CLICK the **File** command and from the File menu SELECT **Save As...** .

3 USE the **Save As...** dialog box to save the blank picture on the Desktop under the name:

Diag1

Activity 13.2 Drawing a diagram

1 CLICK the **Text** tool button, CLICK the drawing area and TYPE in:

Arithmetic & Logic Unit

The effect of doing this is to produce the distorted effect:

```
┌─ ··─┐
│ Arit │
│ hme  │
├ tic & ┤
│ Logi │
│  c   │
└ Unit ┘
   ··
```

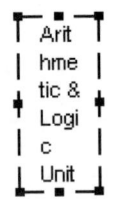

The dotted line around the text contains a number of small squares called *handles*.

2 PLACE the cusor on the bottom right-hand corner handle and the cursor changes to a double-headed arrow pointing diagonally. You may need to be delicate in placing the pointer to achieve this effect.

3 With the double-headed pointer showing DRAG the handle up and to the right.

The box around the text then changes shape to accommodate the text on a single line.

4 CLICK the **Rectangle** tool button and draw a rectangle around the text:

| Arithmetic & Logic Unit |

5 USE the **Select** tool to select the rectangle and then USE the **Edit** command to **Copy** and **Paste** a copy of this recangle onto the drawing area.

6 CLICK the rectangular **Select** tool button and SELECT the copied rectangle.

7 DRAG the selected rectangle to a position just beneath the original rectangle.

8 CLICK the **Eraser** tool button and ERASE the text in the copied rectangle:

| Arithmetic & Logic Unit |

| |

9 CLICK the **Text** tool button and, in a clear area of the screen, TYPE the text:

Control Unit

10 SELECT this text and DRAG it into the empty rectangle.

11 CLICK the **Pencil** tool button, HOLD DOWN the shift key and DRAW two lines between the two rectangles:

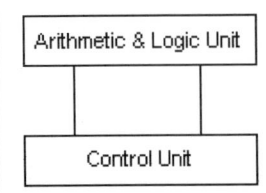

| Arithmetic & Logic Unit |

| Control Unit |

Activity 13.3 Drawing detail into a diagram

1 CLICK the **View** command to reveal a drop-down menu of further commands:

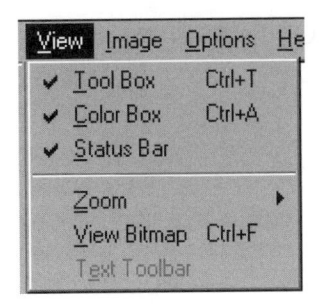

The Zoom command enables the drawing to be magnified so that detail can be added to a drawing more accurately.

2 MOVE the cursor to the **Zoom** command to reveal a further menu of options:

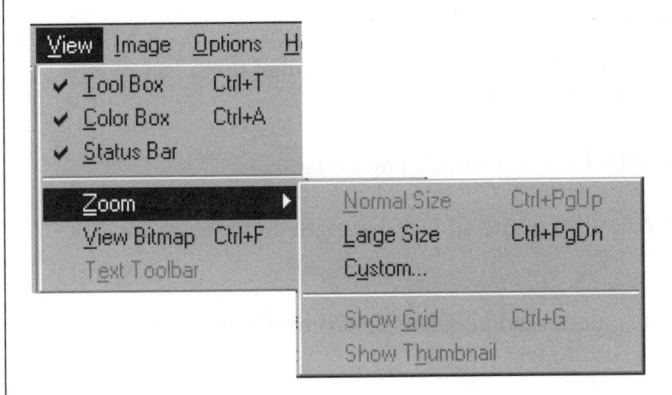

3 CLICK the **Large Size** option and the drawing becomes magnified:

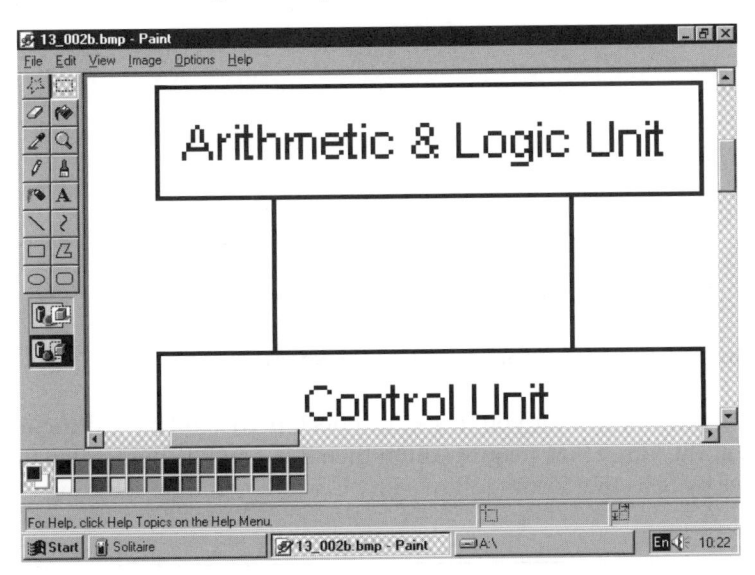

(Again, you may need to use the slider bars to bring the dawing into view). When you draw a line in Paint you are colouring in a sequence of *pixels* (small rectangular shapes). However, these pixels are so small that they cannot be easily distinguished without magnifying the drawing area.

4   ENSURE that **Black** is selected on the colour palette, SELECT the **Pencil** tool and CLICK anywhere on the white area of the drawing:

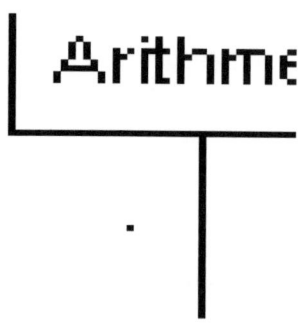

```
Arithme
```

A small black rectangle appears. This is a magnified pixel and you have coloured it in black using the Pencil tool.

5   CLICK the white coloured square on the colour palette to change the selected left-hand mouse button colour from black to white.

6   With the Pencil Tool still selected CLICK the single black pixel.

The pixel disappears. It is in fact coloured white so is indistinguishable from the background.

7   RE-SELECT **Black** on the colour palette and USE the **Pencil** tool to draw in an arrow head on the line joining the two rectangles:

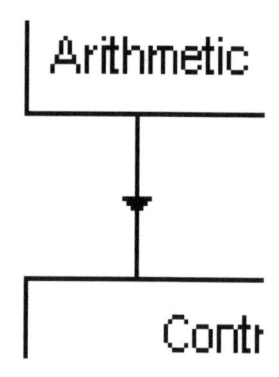

```
Arithmetic

         Contr
```

8   CLICK the **View** command, SELECT **Zoom** followed by **Normal Size**.

The drawing reverts to its original size for you to see the effect. If you still have difficulty colouring in pixels even at the Large Size magnification then it is possible to increase the magnification still further by Selecting Zoom followed by Custom and then selecting 800%.

Activity 13.4 Completing the diagram

1 COMPLETE the diagram until it looks as follows:

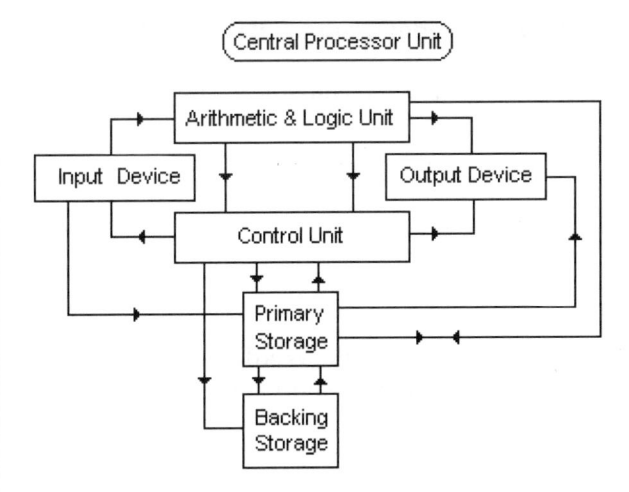

```
                    ( Central Processor Unit )
         ┌──────────────────────────────────────┐
         │      Arithmetic & Logic Unit         │
    ┌────┤                                      ├────┐
    │ Input Device │              │ Output Device │   │
    │              │              │               │   │
    │              │  Control Unit                │   │
    │              │                              │   │
    │              │   Primary                    │   │
    │              │   Storage                    │   │
    │              │                              │   │
    │              │   Backing                    │   │
    │              │   Storage                    │   │
```

To obtain a more precise view of the location of the pixels you can opt to view the magnified drawing against a collection of gridlines.

2 CLICK the **View** command and SELECT **Zoom** followed by Show Grid.

The effect is as follows:

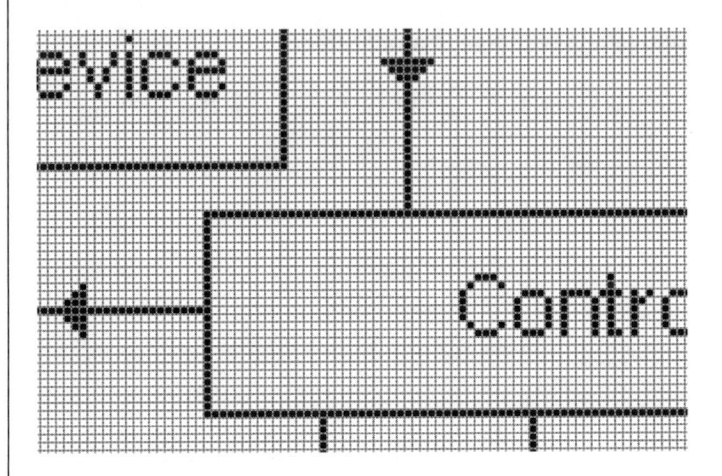

Note: When you saved this file to the desktop Paint added the filename extension .bmp. This means that the file is a BMP file – a particular graphic file recognised by Paint.

Drawing a diagram 55

| Task 14 | ## Using Paint to enhance a WordPad document

▶ **Placing in a WordPad document graphics developed in Paint**

Ensure that the desktop is on display and contains the two icons Doc1 and Diag1.

Activity 14.1 **Capturing an image of the screen**

1 OPEN the **WordPad** accessory

We wish to place in the document Doc1 some elements of the WordPad screen. To do this we must first make a copy of the WordPad screen in memory (on the clipboard).

2 PRESS the **Print Screen** key on the keyboard.

This has sent a copy of the screen that you now see to that reserved part of the memory called the Clipboard.

3 OPEN the **Paint** accessory.

We require to have available as much of the drawing area as possible.

4 CLICK the **Maximize** button to take advantage of a full screen.

5 CLICK the **View** command on the Menu bar and SELECT the Color Box option.

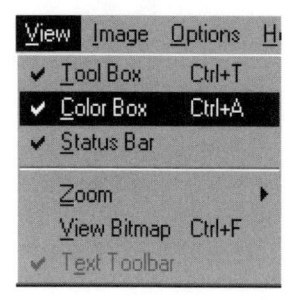

```
View  Image  Options  H
 ✓ Tool Box      Ctrl+T
 ✓ Color Box     Ctrl+A
 ✓ Status Bar

   Zoom              ▶
   View Bitmap   Ctrl+F
 ✓ Text Toolbar
```

This will remove the tick alongside the Color Box option and remove the display of the colour palette thereby giving more room in the drawing area. We could, if we wished, remove the display of the Tool bar but we shall have need of the tools so we shall leave them where they are.

6 CLICK the **Edit** command on the Menu bar and SELECT the **Paste** option from the Edit drop-down menu.

The drawing area then fills with an image of the WordPad screen:

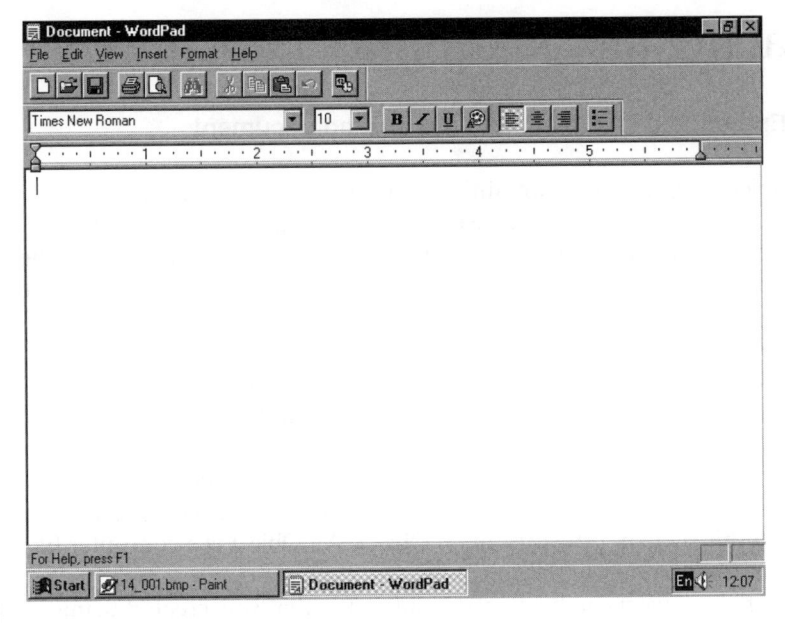

We require only two parts of this display.

7 CLICK the **Select** tool and use the tool to surround the three buttons B, I and U with a dashed-line rectangle.

We have selected just this section of the WordPad display.

8 CLICK the **Edit** command on the Menu bar and SELECT the **Copy** option from the Edit drop-down menu.

9 CLOSE the **Paint** accessory (do not bother to Save it when requested) and OPEN the WordPad document on the desktop by double-clicking the Doc1 icon.

10 When the document appears in the WordPad window PLACE the cursor to the immediate right of Type Style in the Enhancements section of the document.

11 CLICK the **Edit** command and SELECT **Paste**.

The small graphic that you copied from the Paint accessory now appears alongside the text. Indeed, despite the fact that you see it as a picture the WordPad program sees it as a single character.

12 SELECT the graphic by dragging the cursor over it and PRESS **Backspace**.

The graphic disappears. Worry not, you can Paste it back again because you have not lost the copy on the clipboard.

13 REPEAT this insertion procedure and PLACE a copy of the unopened Font list box alongside Type Font and Size in the Doc1 document.

Task 15 | Placing an Object into a document

➤ Embedding an Object into a WordPad document

An Object is a file that maintains a connection with the application package that was used to create the file. For example, if you wished to create a business plan you would probably use a wordprocessor for the text and a spreadsheet for the detailed financial aspects of the plan. The final printed document would then be produced by combining the outputs from each of these two application packages. However, if you wanted the plan to be accessible with a computer so that whomsoever was interested could read the plan at their computer then you would have a problem. If they wanted to read the text then they would have to access the wordprocessor. If they wanted to read the detailed financial forecasting they would have to access the spreadsheet. There is a way around this by using the idea of an Object. An Object is a computer file that maintains a link with the application package that was used to create it. An Object can be placed inside a file that was created using an application package different from the one used for the Object. For example, if a spreadsheet Object were placed inside a wordprocessed document it is possible for the user not only to read the document but also to access the Object from within the document.

For the purposes of this Task we shall assume that the document Doc1 is part of an ongoing project to produce a complete guide to document editing within WordPad. For this reason, you are going to require continual access to the screen dump of the WordPad window that we used to enhance the document in the previous Task. We shall use the screen dump as a Object and insert it into the document.

Activity 15.1 **Creating the Object**

We must first create the file that is going to be the Object. This file will be the screen dump of the WordPad window that will be saved as a BMP file via the Paint accessory.

1 ENSURE that the **WordPad** window is on display

2 PRESS the **Print Screen** key on the keyboard to send a copy of the screen (called a screen dump) to the clipboard.

3 OPEN the **Paint** accessory, MAXIMIZE the window and TURN OFF the Colour Palette display.

4 USE the **Edit** command menu to Paste the screen dump into Paint.

5 SAVE this image to the desktop as a BMP file named WPScreen.

This file is the Object.

Activity 15.2 Embedding the Object

Having created the screen dump we now wish to convert it into an Object and then embed it into the Doc1 document.

1 ENSURE that the desktop is on display

2 OPEN the Doc1 document by double clicking its icon on the desktop and PLACE the text cursor immediately below the title Document Editing.

3 MAXIMIZE the document

4 CLICK the **Insert** command and SELECT the **Object** option to reveal the Insert Object dialog box:

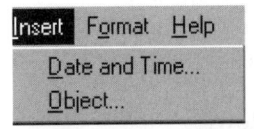

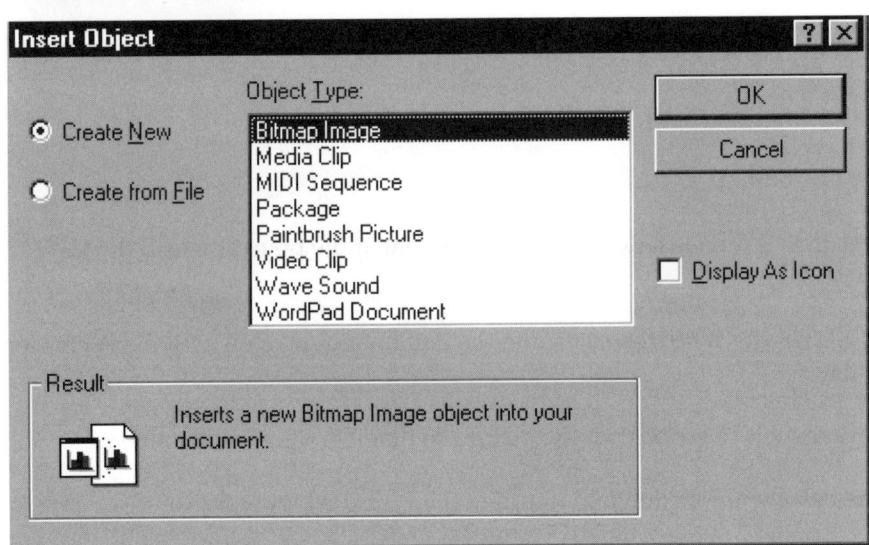

5 CLICK the **Create from File** check box and a **Browse** button appears:

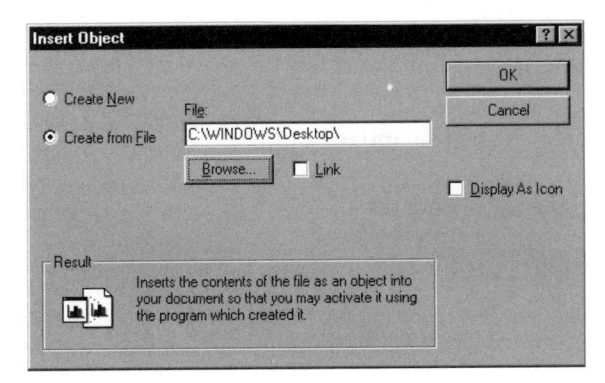

6 CLICK the **Browse** button to reveal the Browse window:

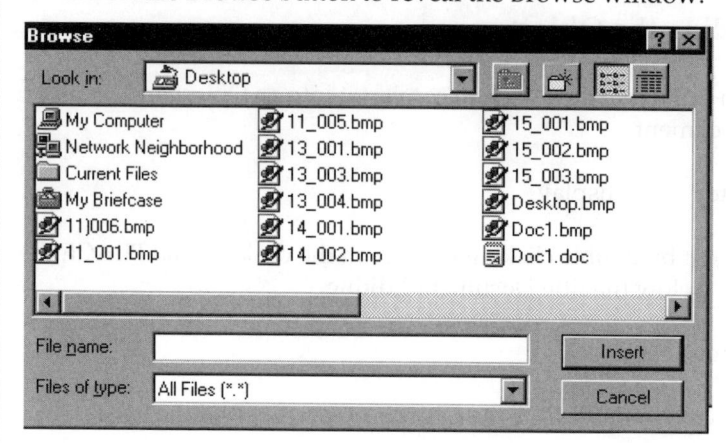

7 CLICK the **Look in** list box arrow to ensure you are looking at the desktop

8 CLICK the **WPScreen** icon in the file display window to select it.

9 CLICK the **Insert** button to RETURN to the **Insert Object** window.

10 CLICK the **Display As Icon** check box.

11 ENSURE that the **Link** check box is empty.

12 CLICK the **OK** button.

The WPScreen icon is then inserted into the document at the point at which the text cursor was located.

13 DOUBLE-CLICK the **WPScreen** icon and the Paint window open with the WPScreen file on display.

14 USE the Brush tools to scribble on the picture so that it is significantly altered.

15 CLOSE the **Paint** window down to return to the WordPad window.

16 CLOSE the **WordPad** window to return to the desktop display.

Activity 15.3 **Manipulating an Object**

1 OPEN **Doc1** from the desktop and CLICK the **Maximize** button

2 CLICK the **WPScreen** icon to reveal the Object handles:

3 DRAG each of the handles in turn to see how the box enclosing the icon changes shape.

4 By pointing inside the box containing the icon DRAG the icon to another part of the document.

The box containing the icon behaves as though it were a single text character and as such can be dragged to any place in the document desired.

5 With the handles on display PRESS the **Backspace** key and the icon disappears.

The Object has been removed.

6 FINISH this *Activity* with all windows closed down and the dektop on display.

Activity 15.4 Linking an Object

1 DOUBLE-CLICK the **WPScreen** icon on the desktop to display the WordPad screen dump in the Paint window.

You will notice that the scribble that you put on its image in the WordPad document is not present in this image. There is no reason why there should be – they are two separate documents. It is, however, possible to create a link whereby the amendment made to the Object in the WordPad document would be reflected in the WRScreen image on the desktop and vice versa.

2 REPEAT the procedure of *Activity 15.2* to PLACE the **WPScreen** icon into Doc1 as an Object with one minor change – in the Insert Object dialog box CLICK the **Link** check box.

Now, when the Object is embedded into the document it retains a link with its image on the desktop.

3 ENSURE that **Doc1** is on display with the WPScreen icon in view.

4 DOUBLE-CLICK in the **WPScreen** icon to display the Paint window with the screen dump on display.

5 USE the **Brush** too to scribble graffiti over the image and then CLICK the **Close** box and close the Object down to its icon.

6 SAVE the changes made to WPScreen.bmp when asked if you wish to.

7 CLOSE the **WordPad** window down and RETURN to the desktop display.

8 DOUBLE-CLICK the **WPScreen** icon on the desktop and when it opens up you will see that the graffiti has also been reflected on this copy of the file – the two images are linked.

If you were now to amend this image it would be reflected in the image stored in the document. Try it.

Section C

File management

Having spent a goodly amount of time and effort using the WordPad and Paint accessories you will by now be well on the way to attaining that familiarity with the GUI that is essential for ease and pleasure of use. One of the many features of the system that you have come across is the file. The document Doc1 that you created in WordPad was a file, the picture that you created in Paint was a file. In fact every icon on the desktop is a file – so what exactly is a file? In this section we shall answer that question and, at the same time, you will learn how files are organized in Windows 95 and how they can be created, saved, moved, copied and deleted.

By extensive use of the Windows 95 Explorer you will learn how to:

- name, access and move files within the system
- use the comprehensive Help facility
- use Find to locate files
- backup files to and restore files from floppy diskette

In addition, you will become more aware of the means whereby Windows 95 stores files and records the locations of files stored within the system. You will also learn to appreciate the need for transferring files from the internal medium of the hard disk to an external medium such as a floppy diskette for safe storage.

Task 16: The Windows 95 Explorer
Task 17: Accessing files from Explorer
Task 18: Moving files from folder to folder
Task 19: Manipulating Help
Task 20: Find
Task 21: Backing up, restoring and comparing files

| Task 16 | # The Windows 95 Explorer

➤ **What computer files are and how they are stored in Windows 95**

Ensure that the desktop is on display.

Activity 16.1 **Files and Explorer**

A file is a collection of information that has been stored on a disk. The information stored could be a complete program, a segment of a program or just simply data such as a document or a drawing. When it is stored on a disk it must be identifiable so that it can be accessed at a later time. To identify the file it is given a name. The name consists of up to 8 alphanumeric characters followed by a dot and then three more alphanumeric characters. For example:

file.txt
document.doc
picture4.bmp

are all permitted names for files. The three characters after the dot are referred to as the filename extension and are often used to identify the type of file. For example:

.txt   is usually used to identify a text file; one that only contains keyboard characters
.doc   is used by many wordprocessors to identify document files
.bmp is used to identify the bit mapped file of a drawing.

1 CLICK the **Start** button and from the Start menu SELECT **Programs**:

2 From the Programs menu SELECT **Windows Explorer** to reveal the Exploring - Hard Disk (C) window

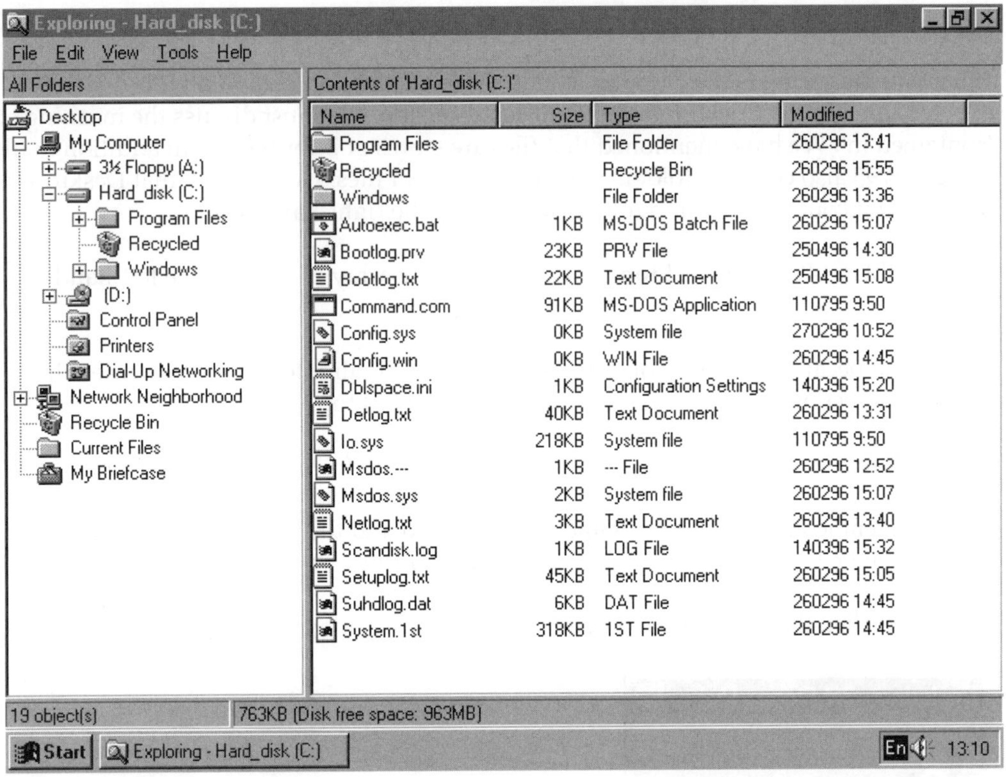

This window contains two sections. The left-hand section is headed All folders and the right-hand section is headed Contents of Desktop.

What you see in the left-hand section is the Desktop icon in the top left-hand corner and hanging from it an array of other icons.

3 DOUBLE-CLICK the **Desktop** icon to change the display as follows:

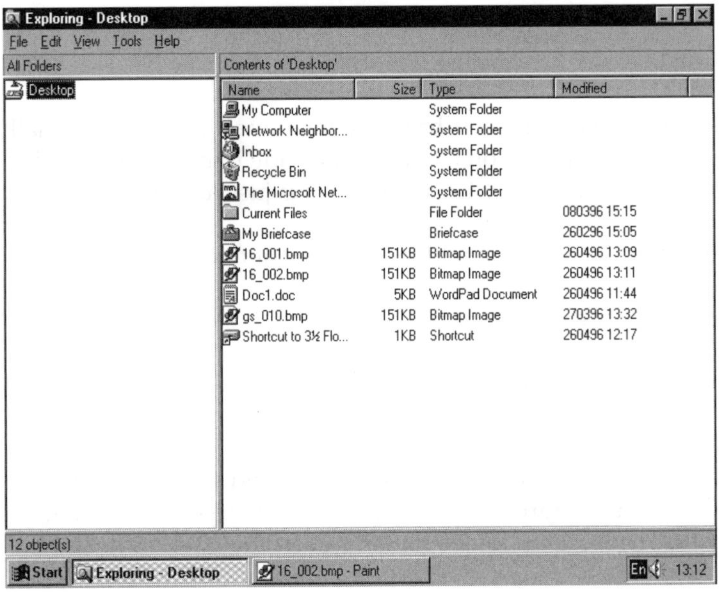

If this was your original display then leave it this way.

What you are seeing is the Desktop icon in the left-hand section and all those files that are contained in the Desktop in the right-hand section. We must discuss the meaning of 'contained in'. We have mentioned that files are stores of information. In addition to files, Windows 95 also contains folders which are stores of files. Here we see that Desktop is a folder and it contains files and folders as listed in the right-hand section.

4 DOUBLE-CLICK the **Desktop** icon to retrieve the array of icons in the left-hand section.

Notice that because the name of the Desktop icon is highlighted in reverse video the right-hand section still displays the contents of the Desktop folder.

5 CLICK in turn each one of the array of icons hanging from the Desktop icon.

As a different icon is clicked, its name is highlighted and the icons in the right-hand section change to reflect the contents of the selected icon.

When you click the $3^1/_2$ (A:\) icon you will reveal a warning window:

```
Exploring - 3½ Floppy (A:)        [X]

  (X)    A:\ is not accessible.
         The device is not ready.

       [ Retry ]    [ Cancel ]
```

This icon represents the programs that activate the external disk drive and if there is no disk in the drive or the disk that is in is unreadable then you will reveal this warning message.

6 CLICK the **Cancel** button to close the warning window.

You will notice that some of the icons in the left-hand section have a + or a – in a small square box alongside the icon name. If an icon has a + alongside it this means that it contains further folders and/or files. The My Computer icon is just such an icon.

7 CLICK the **My Computer** icon to reveal an additional array of folders.

Notice that the + sign has now changed to a – sign.

8 CLICK the **– sign** to the left of the My Computer icon and the additional array of folders disappears.

The way the various folders and files are displayed in the left-hand section of the Explore window demonstrates the hierarchical structure of the storage. It is like big boxes containing little boxes. The Desktop folder contains everything. In particular it contains other folders each of which in turn may contain yet more folders which contain files. The hierarchical structure is called a tree structure because it is akin to branches growing from branches and the whole growing from the root which in this case is the Desktop icon.

Activity 16.2 Exploring Explorer

We can change the way in which files and folders are displayed in the right-hand section of the Explorer window.

1 ENSURE that the Explorer window is on display and occupying the full screen.

2 CLICK the **Accessories** icon (inside the Program Files folder in the Hard Disk (C:) folder) to display all the associated files and folders in the right-hand section.

3 CLICK the **View** command to reveal a drop-down menu of further commands:

```
View  Tools  Help
   Toolbar
 ✓ Status Bar

   Large Icons
   Small Icons
   List
 • Details

   Arrange Icons  ▶
   Line up Icons

   Refresh
   Options...
```

4 SELECT **Large** Icons and the right-hand display changes to accommodate the larger icons.

5 CLICK the **View** command and SELECT **Small** icons to revert to a display similar to the default display except the icons are now arranged across the screen in rows rather than down the screen in columns.

6 CLICK the **View** command and SELECT **List** to retrieve the default display.

7 CLICK the **View** command and SELECT **Details**.

Alongside each file is its size in bytes, its type and the date when it was last amended.

8 CLICK the **View** command and SELECT **Arrange Icons** to reveal a futher list of options:

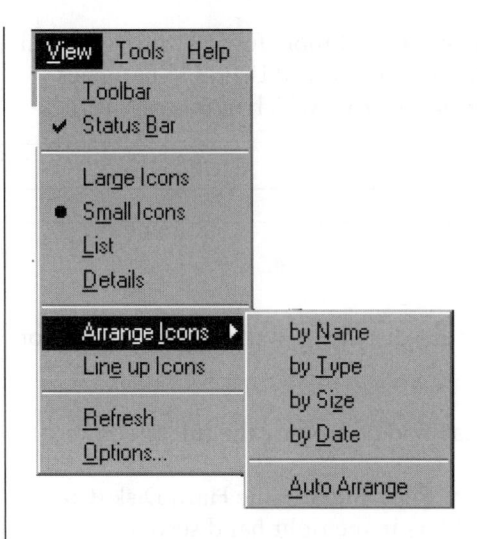

9 SELECT each of the options in turn to see the effect on the listing arrangement.

10 CLICK the **View** command and SELECT **Options** to reveal the Options dialog box:

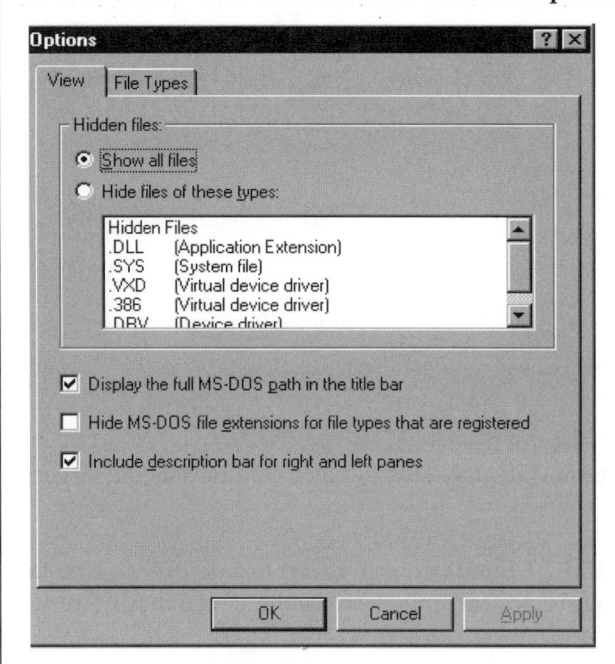

11 In the View card ELECT to **Show all files, Display the Full MS-DOS path** and **Include Description bar for right and left panes**.

12 CLICK the **OK** button to close this dialog box and in the right-hand section the legend

Contents of 'C:\Program Files\Accessories'

appears in the Description bar above.

68 File management

> **Exploring - C:\Program Files\Accessories**
> File Edit View Tools Help
> All Folders | Contents of 'C:\Program Files\Accessories'

This is the path of the Accessories folder and it is telling you that the Accessories folder is contained inside a folder of Program Files which is stored on the C drive – the hard disk.

Activity 16.3 Creating a new folder

1 ENSURE that the Explorer window is on display

2 CLICK on the **Desktop** icon to select it

3 CLICK the **File** command to reveal a drop-down list of further options:

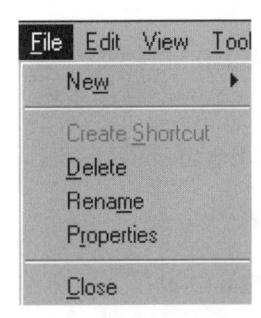

> File Edit View Tool
> New ▶
> Create Shortcut
> Delete
> Rename
> Properties
> Close

4 SELECT **New** and from the further options SELECT **Folder**:

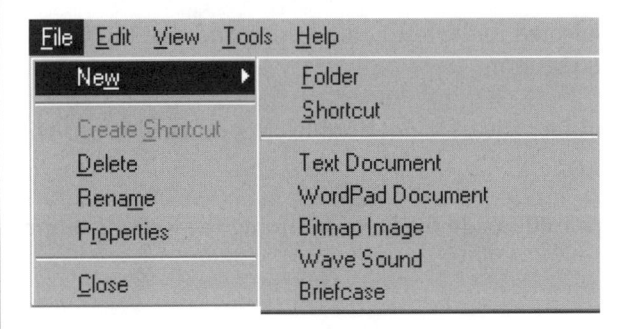

> File Edit View Tools Help
> New ▶   Folder
>   Shortcut
> Create Shortcut
> Delete   Text Document
> Rename   WordPad Document
> Properties   Bitmap Image
>   Wave Sound
> Close   Briefcase

The folder automatically appears in both the left- and right-hand sections with the name New Folder:

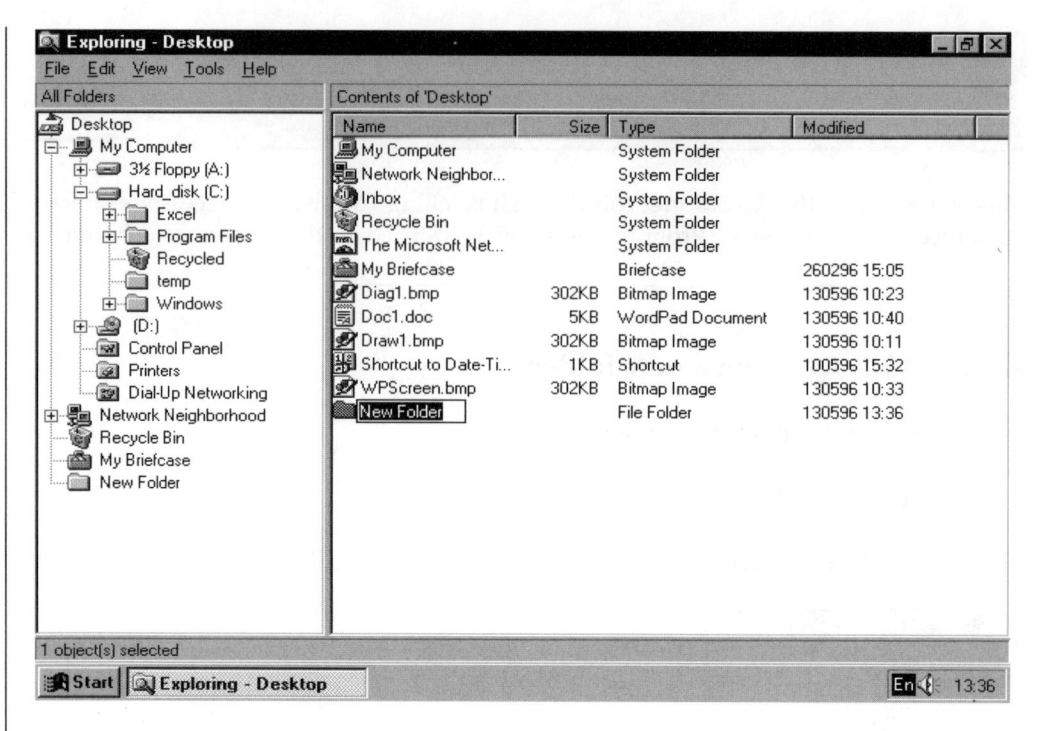

Exploring - Desktop				
File Edit View Tools Help				
All Folders	Contents of 'Desktop'			
	Name	Size	Type	Modified
Desktop	My Computer		System Folder	
My Computer	Network Neighbor...		System Folder	
3½ Floppy (A:)	Inbox		System Folder	
Hard_disk (C:)	Recycle Bin		System Folder	
Excel	The Microsoft Net...		System Folder	
Program Files	My Briefcase		Briefcase	260296 15:05
Recycled	Diag1.bmp	302KB	Bitmap Image	130596 10:23
temp	Doc1.doc	5KB	WordPad Document	130596 10:40
Windows	Draw1.bmp	302KB	Bitmap Image	130596 10:11
(D:)	Shortcut to Date-Ti...	1KB	Shortcut	100596 15:32
Control Panel	WPScreen.bmp	302KB	Bitmap Image	130596 10:33
Printers	New Folder		File Folder	130596 13:36
Dial-Up Networking				
Network Neighborhood				
Recycle Bin				
My Briefcase				
New Folder				
1 object(s) selected				
Start	Exploring - Desktop		En	13:36

5 CLOSE the **Explorer** window and there you will see on the desktop the new folder.

6 DRAG and DROP the **Doc1** and **WPScreen** icons into the folder.

The icons disappear form the desktop display because they are in the folder.

7 RE-OPEN the **Explorer** window

8 ENSURE that the Desktop icon is selected in the left-hand section and that the New Folder is displayed in the right-hand section.

9 Carefully CLICK the name **New Folder** twice. Do not double-click otherwise you will open up the folder.

You will see that a text cursor has appeared inside the box containing the folder's name which is itself highlighted.

10 TYPE a new name at the keyboard:

Current Folder

11 CLICK elsewhere in the Explorer window so as to establish the name change.

Notice that the name has also changed in the left-hand section.

12 CLOSE the **Explorer** window when you will see the name of the new folder changed to the new name on the desktop. It is possible to perform this re-naming process on the desktop itself.

| Task 17 | # Accessing files from Explorer

> **To find specific files from within Explorer**

Ensure that the Explorer window is on display.

Activity 17.1 **Accessing Notepad from Explorer**

Notepad is an Accessory and as such can be accessed via the Start Button on the desktop. However, we shall access it via its icon in the Explorer window.

1. CLICK the **Desktop** icon in the left-hand section until the array of folders and files are seen to hang from it.

2. LOCATE the **Programs** folder and within that the **Accessories** folder.

3. CLICK the **Accessories** folder in the left-hand section to reveal the contents of the folder in the right-hand section.

You will notice that there are only a few files and folders present. This is because this particular Accessories icon does not display the entire contents of the Accessories folder.

4. In the left-hand pane CLICK the **Windows** folder and then the **Start Menu** folder.

You will see that the Start Menu folder contains a second copy of the Programs icon.

5. CLICK this **Programs** icon to reveal, amongst other icons, a second copy of the Accessories icon.

6. CLICK this copy of the **Accessories** icon to reveal all those files and folders that were not present when you opened the previous Accessories icon.

Amongst the contents of the Accesories icon is a file called Notepad.

7. DOUBLE-CLICK the **Notepad** icon displayed in the right-hand section to reveal the Notepad window:

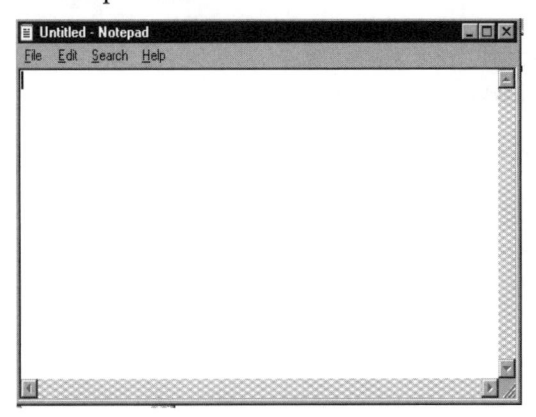

```
┌─────────────────────────────────────┐
│ 📄 Untitled - Notepad      _ □ ✕   │
│ File  Edit  Search  Help            │
├─────────────────────────────────────┤
│ |                                   │
│                                     │
│                                     │
│                                     │
│                                     │
│                                     │
│                                     │
│                                     │
└─────────────────────────────────────┘
```

Notepad is a text editor that facilitates the entry of simple, unenhanced and unformatted text; it is just what its name implies – a notepad for jottings and reminders.

8   ENTER the following text into Notepad:

Find me if you can

9   SAVE this small piece of text in a file called Newnote in the Current Files folder:

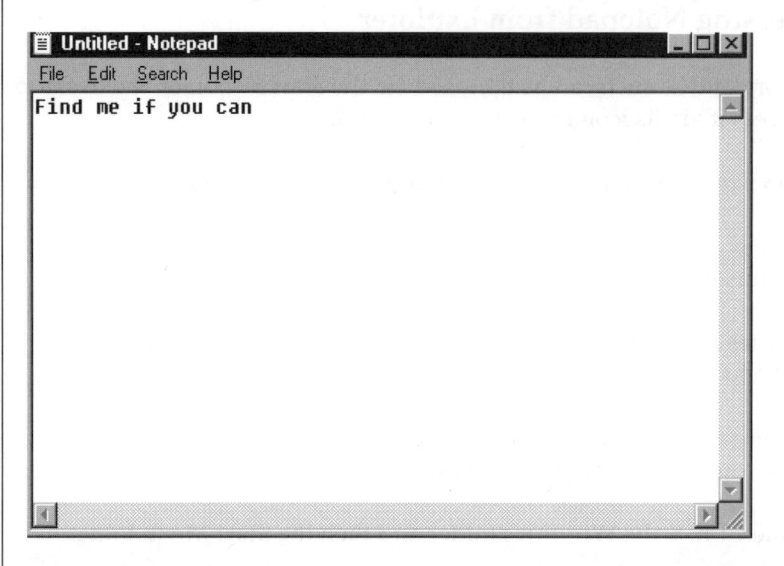

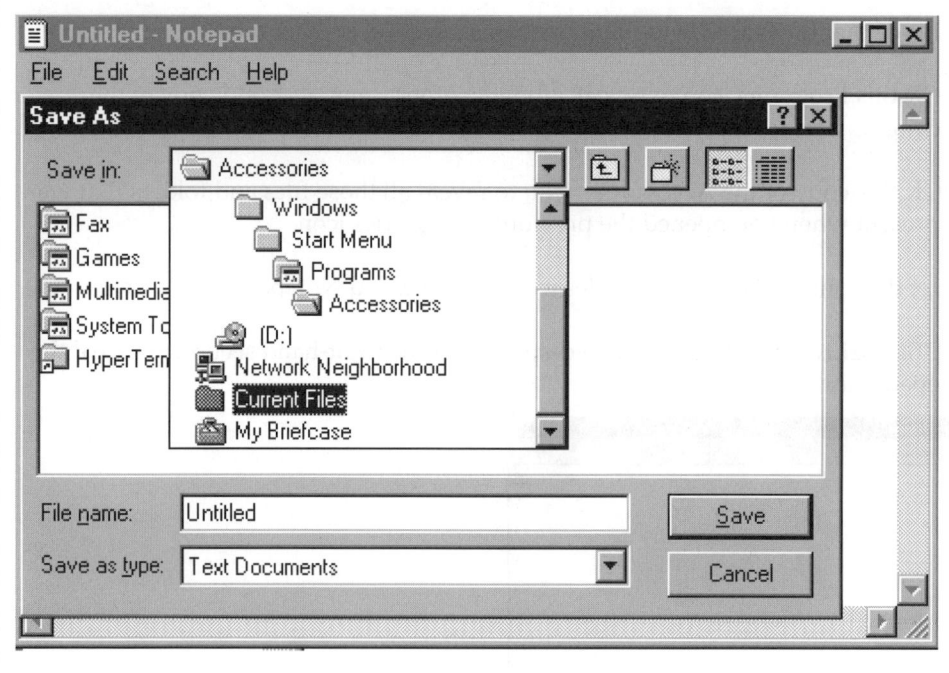

Activity 17.2 Using Find from Explorer

Within Windows 95 is a search utility that permits the user to locate specified files within the plethora of files that constitute the complete system. Ensure that the Exporer window is on display.

1. CLICK the **Tools** command on the Menu bar and from the drop-down menu SELECT **Find**:

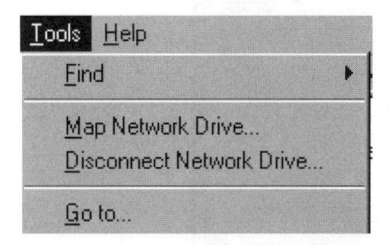

2. From the list of displayed alternatives SELECT **Files or Folders**:

This reveals the Find: All Files dialog box:

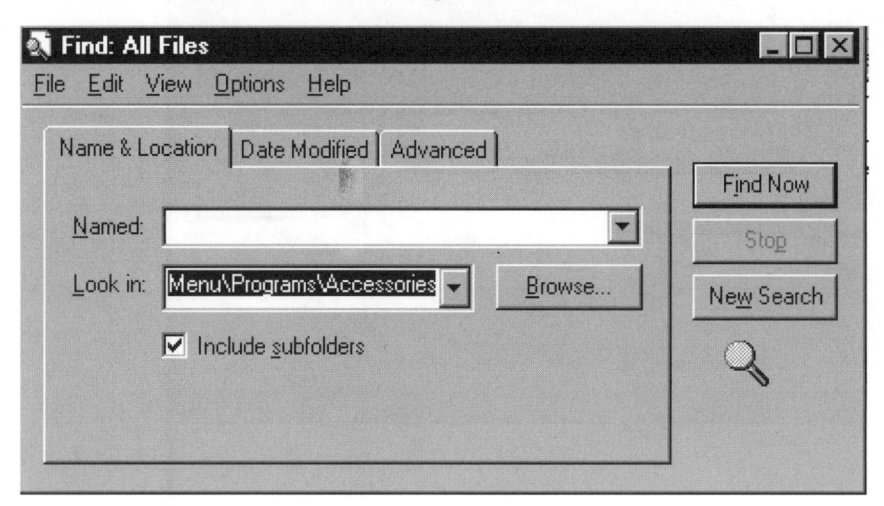

3. ENTER the name of the file to find, **Newnote**.

4. ENTER the Look in as Hard disk (C:) and CLICK the **Find Now** button.

Eventually, the file is located and its address given in the bottom box. An additional feature permits all those files to be found that contain a given piece of text.

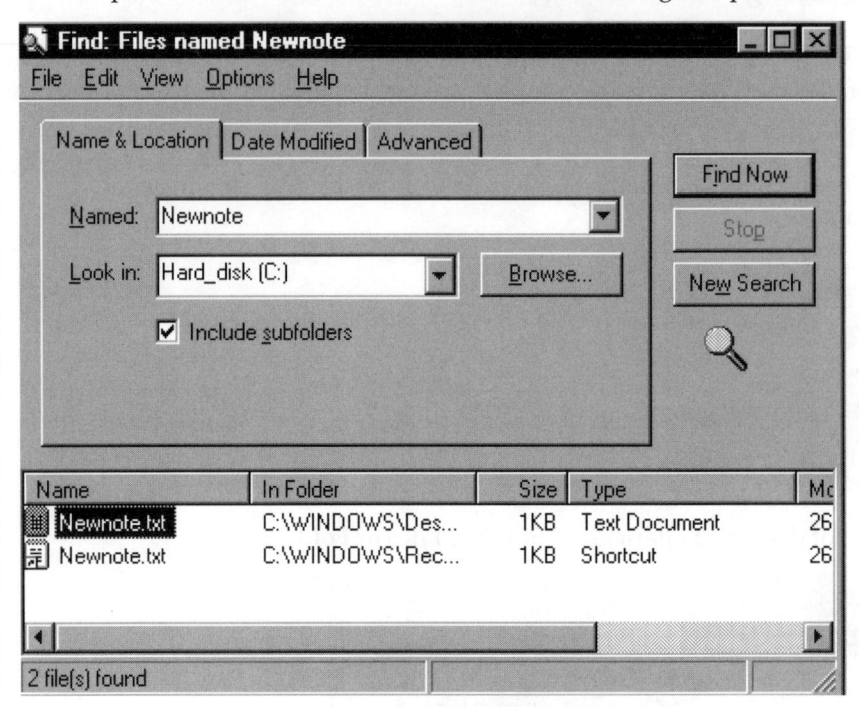

5 CLICK the **Advanced** tab to reveal the Advanced dialog box:

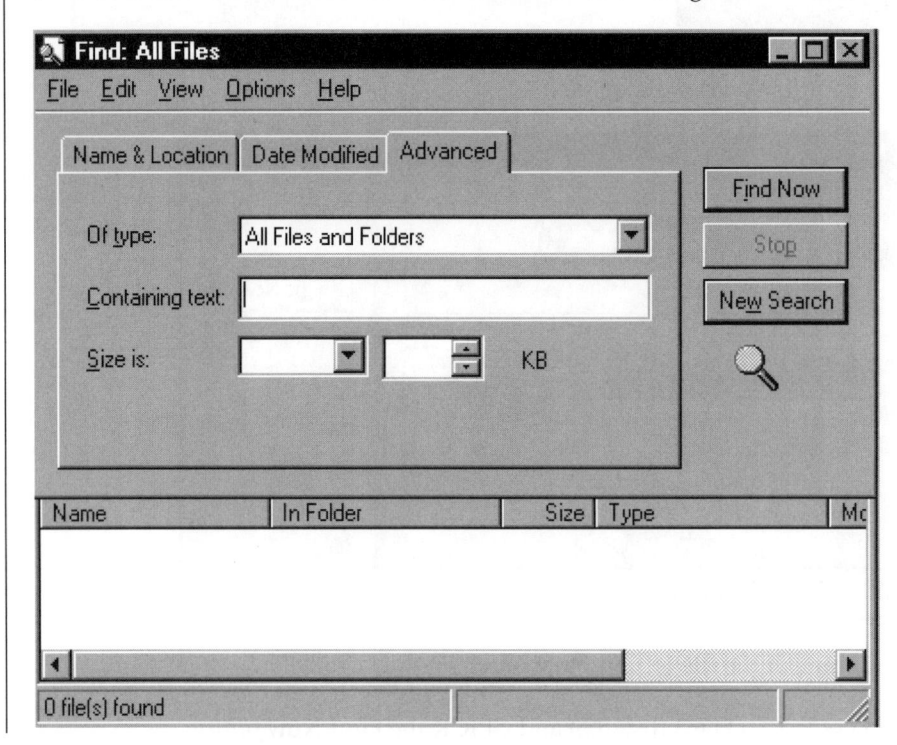

6 CLICK the **list box** to identify exactly what you wish to search:

   All Files and Folders

7 ENTER the content to look for:

   Find me if you can

8 CLICK the **Find Now** button and the system looks through all the files and lists all those files that contain this piece of text.

Not surprisingly, there is just one; Newnote.

Task 18 — Moving files from folder to folder

➤ **Re-locating a file or folder within another folder or disk**

Ensure that the Windows 95 Explorer is on display and that you have available a floppy diskette. It does not matter if the diskette is unformatted because we shall perform the formatting in the next but one Activity.

Activity 18.1 **Moving the Newnotes file to a new folder**

1 CREATE a new folder called:

Work

located inside the Windows folder.

2 LOCATE and CLICK the **Current Files** folder to display its contents.

3 DRAG and DROP the **Newnotes** icon into the Work folder.

The Newnotes file has now been re-located in the Work folder.

4 CLICK the **Work** folder to display its contents in the right-hand section of the Explorer window.

Activity 18.2 **Formatting a floppy diskette**

Every file that you create and save is stored on the computer's hard disk. Whilst hard disks are extremely reliable it is not unknown for them to fail causing all the information stored on them to be lost. Consequently, it is a wise computer user who regularly makes copies of important files to an alternative storage medium by using the external floppy disk drive.

Before a floppy disk can be used it has to be formatted – the magnetic coating on the surface of the disk has to be magnetically marked out into numbered rings and sectors.

Ensure that the desktop is on display.

1 PLACE an unformatted floppy diskette into the external disk drive.

2 DOUBLE-CLICK the **My Computer** icon to reveal the My Computer window:

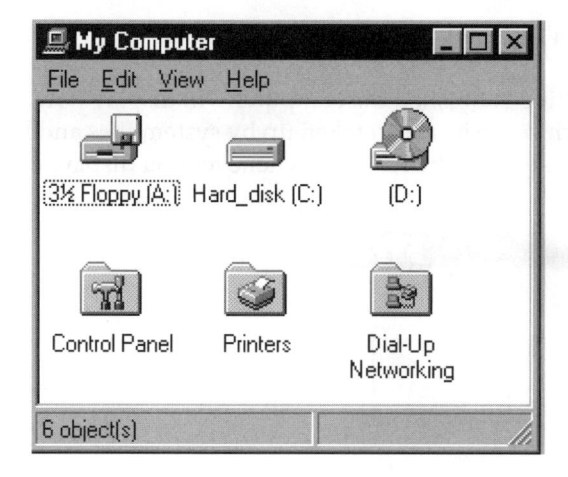

3 CLICK the **3¹/₂ Floppy (A:)** icon to highlight it and, thereby, select it.

Be careful that you do not double-click the icon because if you do you will open the floppy disk folder which will prevent it being formatted.

4 CLICK the **File** command on the Menu bar to reveal a drop-down menu of further options:

5 SELECT **Format** to reveal the Format - 3¹/₂ Floppy (A:) window.

6 ENSURE that the Capacity matches your diskette and CLICK the **Full** radio button.

The Full option scans the disk for any bad sectors on the disk after it has been formatted. The Quick (erase) option is only to be used with a disk that has been formatted previously.

7 ENTER the Label as:

Disk 1

Moving files from folder to folder 77

8 CLICK the **Display summary when finished** check box.

This will ensure that when the formatting is finished the computer will display how much space is available and how much space has been taken up by system files and bad sectors. In addition, the disk will be identifiable by its Label whenever you display its contents.

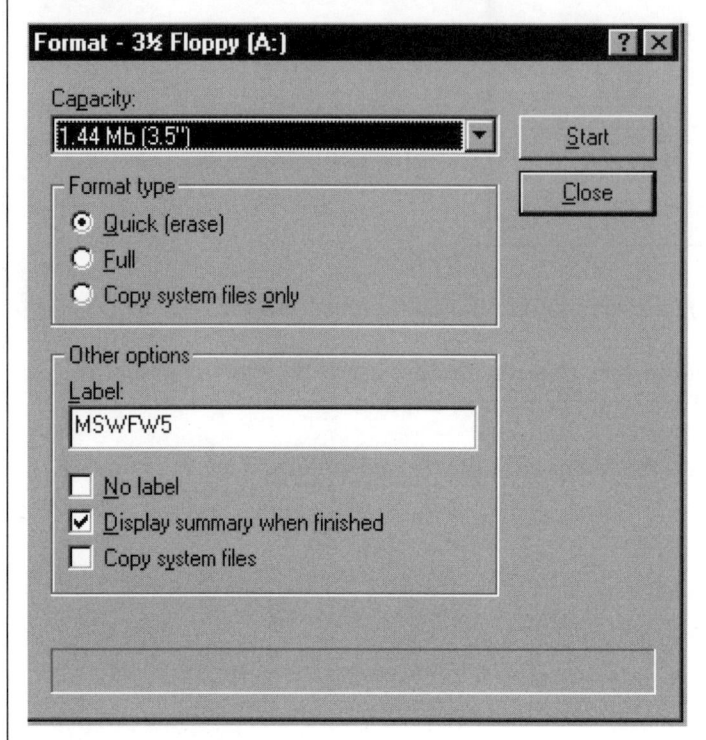

```
Format - 3½ Floppy (A:)                        ? X

Capacity:
[1.44 Mb (3.5")                ▼]      Start

 Format type                           Close
  ⊙ Quick (erase)
  ○ Full
  ○ Copy system files only

 Other options
  Label:
  [MSWFW5              ]

  □ No label
  ☑ Display summary when finished
  □ Copy system files
```

9 CLICK the **Start** button and the floppy diskette in drive A is formatted in readiness for future file storage.

Activity 18.3 Copying a file to a floppy diskette

1 ENSURE that the desktop is on display.

2 PLACE the floppy diskette in the external drive.

3 OPEN the **My Computer** window.

You are going to copy Doc1, which is stored in the Current Files folder on the desktop, onto the floppy diskette in the external drive.

4 OPEN the **Current Files** window.

5 DRAG either or both the **Current Files** window and the **My Computer** window into such a position that you can simultaneously view the Doc1 file in Current Files and the Disk Drive A icon in My Computer.

6 CLICK the **Current Files** window to make it the active window.

7 DRAG the **Doc1** icon from the Current Files window and SUPERIMPOSE it on top of the Disk Drive A icon in the My Computer window.

8 RELEASE the mouse button and the file Doc1 is copied to the floppy disk:

Doc1.doc
Shortcut (2) to
3½ Floppy (A)

Notice, it is copied, not moved – the Doc1 icon still remains in the Current Files folder.

9 DOUBLE-CLICK the **3^1/$_2$ Floppy (A:)** icon in the My Computer window to open the A:\ window where you will see that the file icon Doc1 is on display.

Activity 18.4 Deleting a file from a floppy diskette

We have already seen how to delete a file that is stored on the hard disk. We merely drag and drop its icon into the Recycle bin where it will remain until we decide either to empty the bin or to retrieve the file from the bin. Deleting a file from a floppy diskette is a little different.

1 PLACE the floppy diskette containing the Doc1 file into the external drive.

2 OPEN the **My Computer** window and DOUBLE-CLICK the **3^1/$_2$ Floppy (A:)** icon to open the A:\ window.

3 DRAG the **Doc1** icon to the Recycle bin.

When you release the mouse button a Confirm window appears:

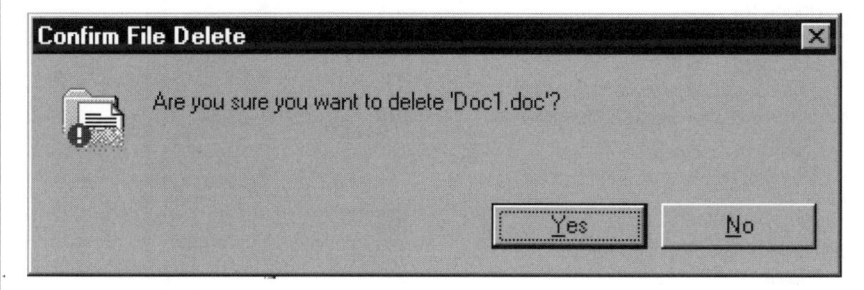

Confirm File Delete

Are you sure you want to delete 'Doc1.doc'?

Yes   No

When you proceed to delete a file from a floppy diskette you do not have the facility to store the file in the Recycle bin until you decide that you really do want to delete it. With a floppy diskette you must be sure that you want to delete it when you place the file icon in the bin.

4 CLICK the **Yes** button and file is deleted.

| Task 19 | # Manipulating Help

> **Using the Help facility to its fullest advantage**

Ensure that the desktop is on display

Activity 19.1 **Viewing the range of Help available**

We have already seen how to access Help in both the Getting Started section and Task 2. However, there, we were primarily concerned with specific Help advice. Here we shall look at the Help facility in detail to see exactly the range of assistance that it offers.

1 CLICK the **Start** button and SELECT **Help** to reveal the Help dialog box:

You will notice that there are three sections to this Help window, Contents, Index and Find.

2 CLICK the **Index** tab to bring the Index dialog box to the fore:

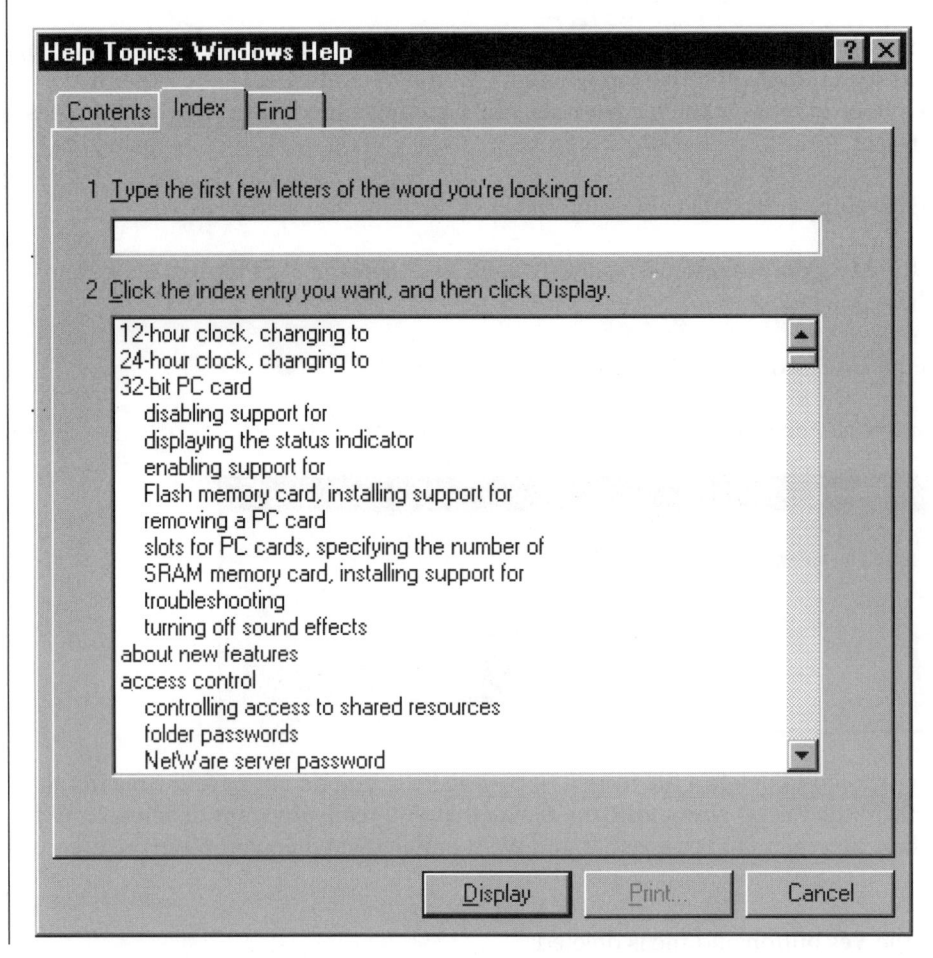

```
Help Topics: Windows Help                                    ? X

 Contents | Index | Find |

  1 Type the first few letters of the word you're looking for.
    [                                                    ]

  2 Click the index entry you want, and then click Display.
    ┌─────────────────────────────────────────────────┬─┐
    │ 12-hour clock, changing to                      │▲│
    │ 24-hour clock, changing to                      │ │
    │ 32-bit PC card                                  │ │
    │     disabling support for                       │ │
    │     displaying the status indicator             │ │
    │     enabling support for                        │ │
    │     Flash memory card, installing support for   │ │
    │     removing a PC card                          │ │
    │     slots for PC cards, specifying the number of│ │
    │     SRAM memory card, installing support for    │ │
    │     troubleshooting                             │ │
    │     turning off sound effects                   │ │
    │ about new features                              │ │
    │ access control                                  │ │
    │     controlling access to shared resources      │ │
    │     folder passwords                            │ │
    │     NetWare server password                     │▼│
    └─────────────────────────────────────────────────┴─┘

              [ Display ]   [ Print... ]   [ Cancel ]
```

In the box numbered 1 you are requested to type in the word correcponding to the specific Help you are looking for and in the lower panel is an alphabetical listing of all the Help topics that are available. The choice is yours, you can either browse the Help topics using the scroll bar at the side of the bottom panel or, much more quickly, you can type in a key word.

3 In the box numbered 1 TYPE:

Help

In the bottom panel you will find that the Help topics have automatically scrolled and the word Help has been selected, that is, it is highlighted.

4 CLICK the **Display** button to reveal a Topics Found window:

This window is listing all those topics on which help can be found.

5 CLICK the **question mark** adjacent to the Close button on the Title bar and a question mark becomes attached to the pointer.

6 CLICK in the centre of the bottom panel and a small window opens describing the purpose of the panel:

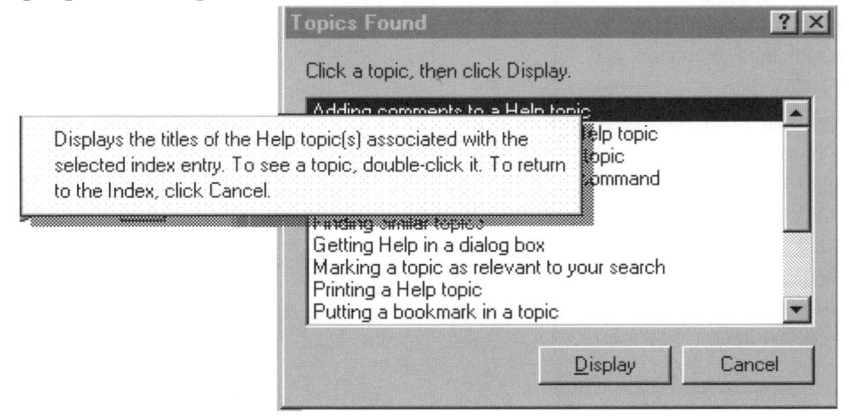

Manipulating Help 81

7 CLICK in the panel and this window and the pointer question mark disappears.

8 CLICK the **question mark** again and this time CLICK the **Display** button.

```
Topics Found                                    [?][X]

Click a topic, then click Display.

  Adding comments to a Help topic
  Changing the font or color of a Help topic
  Copying information from a Help topic
  Displaying help for an MS-DOS command
  Finding a topic in Help
  Finding similar topics
  Getting Help in a dialog box
  Marking a topic as relevant to your search
  Printing a Help topic
  Putting a bookmark in a topic

                         Display      Cancel
     Displays the Help topic you selected.
```

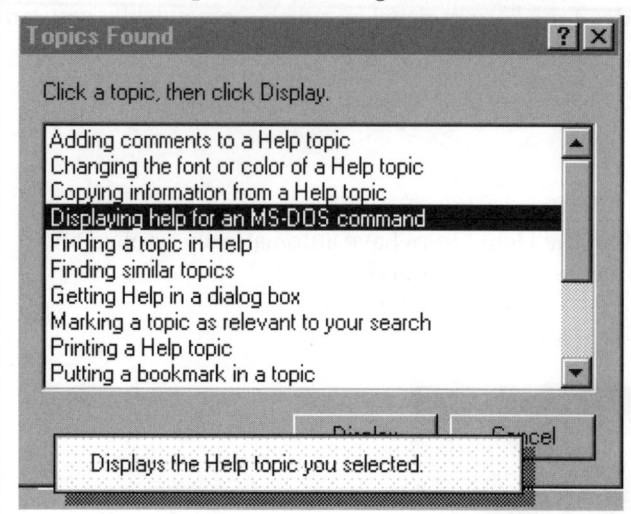

The question mark appears on all the Help windows and can be used to obtain information pertinent to that window.

9 CLICK the **slider** at the right-hand side to view the range of topics and until:

Tips: Using Help

comes into view.

10 SELECT **Tips: Using Help** by highlighting it

11 CLICK the **Display** button and the Help window appears.

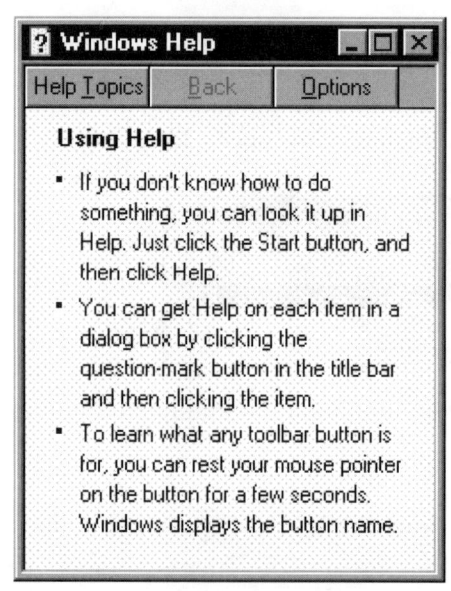

```
Windows Help                         [_][□][X]

 Help Topics   Back      Options

  Using Help

  • If you don't know how to do
    something, you can look it up in
    Help. Just click the Start button, and
    then click Help.

  • You can get Help on each item in a
    dialog box by clicking the
    question-mark button in the title bar
    and then clicking the item.

  • To learn what any toolbar button is
    for, you can rest your mouse pointer
    on the button for a few seconds.
    Windows displays the button name.
```

Read and digest the information in this window as it deals with accessing the Help facility. When you have read this information close all the various windows that are open to leave the desktop on display.

Activity 19.2 The Help Contents

1 CLICK the **Start** button and SELECT **Help**.

2 CLICK the **Contents** tab in the Help window to reveal the Contents dialog box:

![Help Topics: Windows Help dialog box showing Contents tab with categories: If you've used Windows before, Introducing Windows, How To..., Tips and Tricks, Troubleshooting]

Here we see the Help facility listed by category.

3 CLICK the **Tips and Tricks** category and then CLICK the **Open** button (you could have double-clicked the category to produce the same effect) to reveal a list of topics in that category:

📖 **Tips and Tricks**
  📚 For Setting Up the Desktop Efficiently
  📚 For Maintaining Your Computer
  📚 For Running Programs
  📚 For Working with Files and Folders
  📚 For Printing
  📚 For Networking
  📚 Tips of the Day

4 DOUBLE-CLICK the topic:

   For Working with Files and Folders

5 DOUBLE-CLICK the item:

   Putting part of a document on the desktop

   to reveal the Help window:

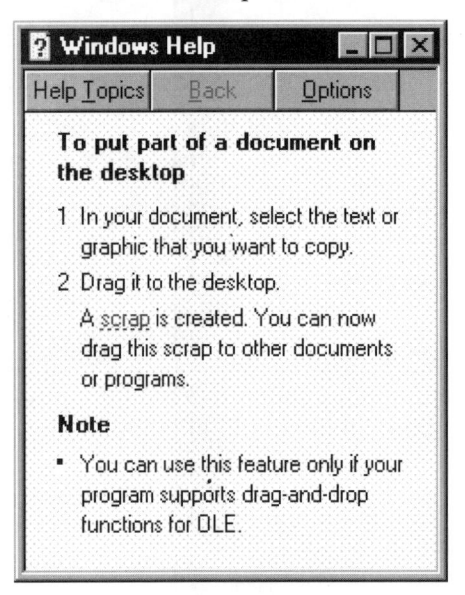

```
┌─────────────────────────────────────┐
│ ❓ Windows Help          _ □ ✕      │
├─────────────────────────────────────┤
│ │Help Topics│  Back    │ Options │  │
├─────────────────────────────────────┤
│ To put part of a document on        │
│ the desktop                         │
│                                     │
│ 1 In your document, select the text │
│   or graphic that you want to copy. │
│ 2 Drag it to the desktop.           │
│   A scrap is created. You can now   │
│   drag this scrap to other documents│
│   or programs.                      │
│                                     │
│ Note                                │
│ • You can use this feature only if  │
│   your program supports drag-and-   │
│   drop functions for OLE.           │
└─────────────────────────────────────┘
```

You will notice that in this description of how to copy a portion of a document onto the desktop the word scrap is in a different colour and is underlined. This means that it is an access point to further information.

6 CLICK the word **scrap** and a small window opens in which is described the meaning of the term scrap.

   ┌─────────────────────────────────────┐
   │ A scrap is a file that is created   │
   │ when you drag part of a document to │
   │ the desktop.   │
   └─────────────────────────────────────┘

7 READ the Help message on how to create a scrap and place the first paragraph of the document Doc1 onto the desktop.

8 COMPLETE this *Activity* with all windows closed and the desktop on display.

Activity 19.3 Manipulating Help windows

You may have noticed that when a Help window was opened, any other window that was subsequently opened stayed behind the Help window. This can be awkward, especially if you want to access a section of a window that is covered by a Help window.

1 OPEN the **Help** window from the **Start** button.

2 CLICK the **Index** tab

3 DOUBLE-CLICK the 12-hour clock:

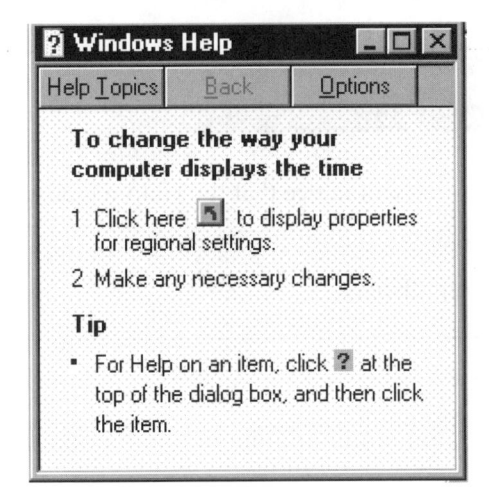

2 CLICK the **Options** command on the Menu bar to reveal a drop-down list of options:

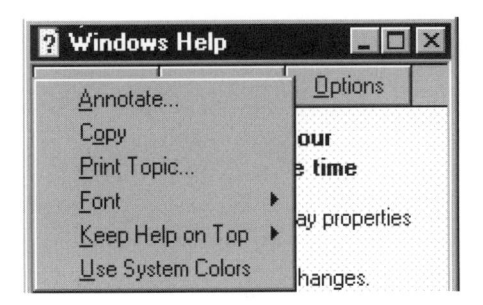

3 SELECT **Keep Help on Top** to reveal a further list of options:

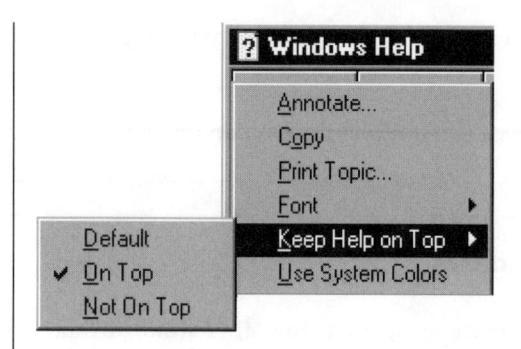

4 SELECT **Not on Top**

The Options menu closes and now if you open a window you can move it in front of an open Help window.

5 OPEN **Doc1** from the desktop

Doc1 opens and is behind the Help window:

6 USE the Task bar to switch applications when you will notice that the Help window is now behind the Doc1 window.

7 CLICK the Close button to return to the desktop display.

| Task 20 | # Find

> **The extensive Find facility provided with the Help facility**

Ensure that the desktop is on display

Activity 20.1 The Find dialog box

1 OPEN the **Help** window from the Start button and CLICK the **Find** tab to reveal the Find dialog box:

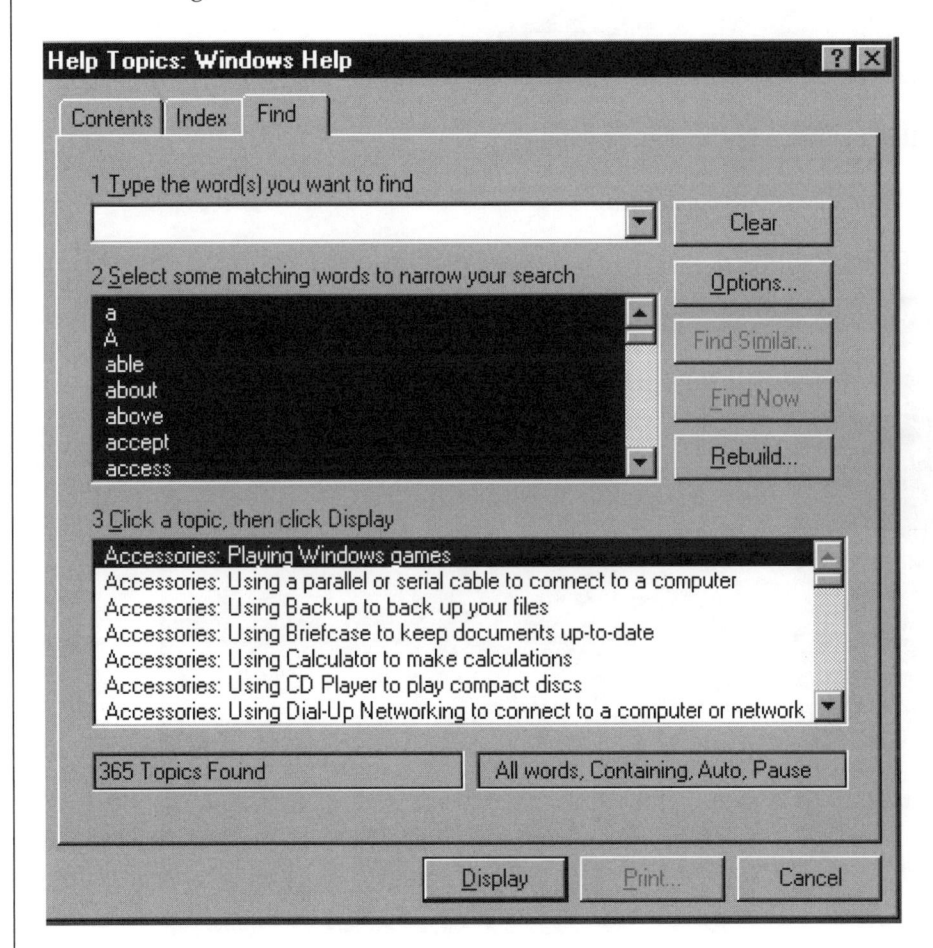

```
Help Topics: Windows Help                                    ? X

 Contents | Index | Find |

 1 Type the word(s) you want to find
 [                                    ▼]    [ Clear    ]

 2 Select some matching words to narrow your search   [ Options... ]
 ┌────────────────────────────────────┐▲
 │ a                                  │    [ Find Similar... ]
 │ A                                  │
 │ able                               │    [ Find Now ]
 │ about                              │
 │ above                              │
 │ accept                             │    [ Rebuild... ]
 │ access                             ▼
 └────────────────────────────────────┘

 3 Click a topic, then click Display
 ┌────────────────────────────────────┐▲
 │ Accessories: Playing Windows games                       │
 │ Accessories: Using a parallel or serial cable to connect to a computer │
 │ Accessories: Using Backup to back up your files          │
 │ Accessories: Using Briefcase to keep documents up-to-date│
 │ Accessories: Using Calculator to make calculations       │
 │ Accessories: Using CD Player to play compact discs       │
 │ Accessories: Using Dial-Up Networking to connect to a computer or network ▼
 └────────────────────────────────────┘

 [ 365 Topics Found          ]    [ All words, Containing, Auto, Pause ]

                    [ Display ]   [ Print... ]   [ Cancel ]
```

Before this facility can be used a list of words and topics has to be created. This may already have been done for you but we shall assume that it has not.

2 CLICK the **Rebuild** button to reveal the Find Setup Wizard:

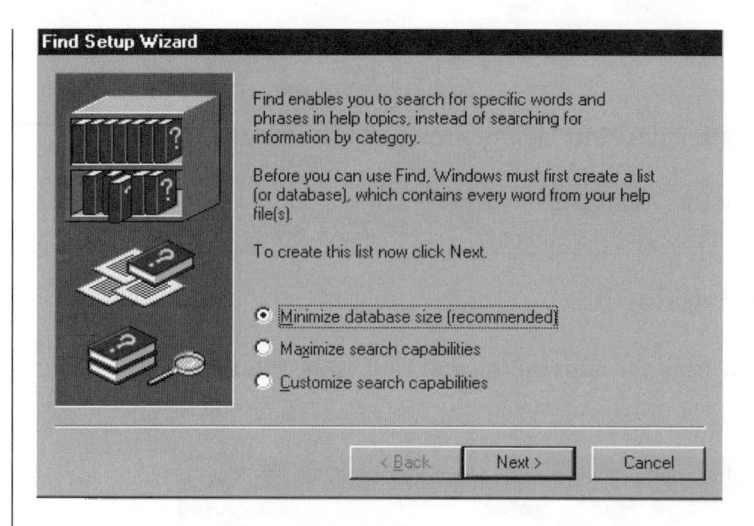

3 CLICK the first radio button annotated:

   Minimize database size (recommended)

4 CLICK the **Next** button to reveal an information window:

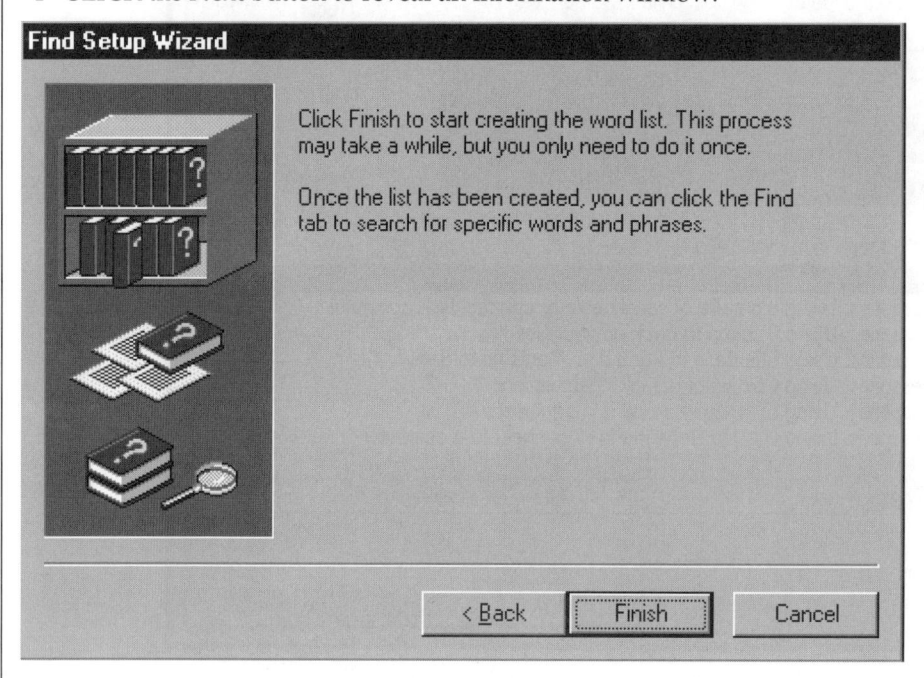

5 CLICK the **Finish** button and a Create Word List... window appears as the system creates the word list.

When the cunstruction of the word list is complete you are returned to the Find dialog box. We must now decide on the structure of the search and which files we wish to include in any of our searches.

6   CLICK the **Options...** button to reveal the Options dialog box:

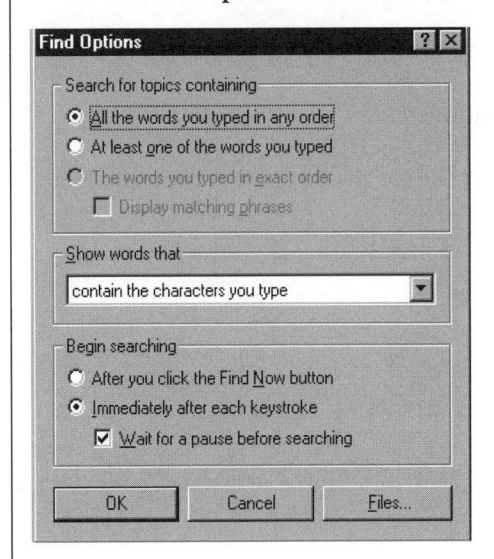

7   CLICK the first radio button annotated:

   All the words you typed in any order

   in the Search for topics containing box.

8   From the list box annotated Show words that SELECT:

   begin with the characters you type

9   Click the radio button annotated:

   Immediately after each keystroke

10 CLICK the **Files** button to reveal the Select Files to Search dialog box:

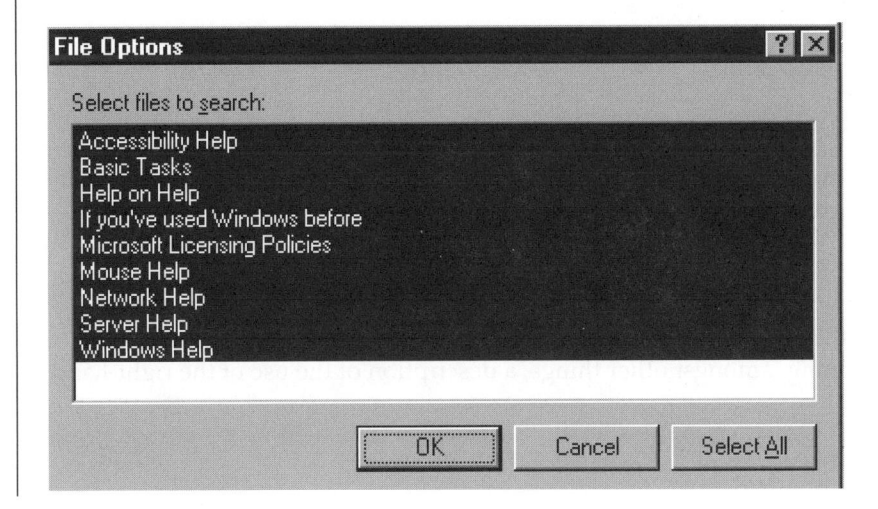

11 CLICK the **Select All** button to highlight all the types of files.

12 CLICK the **OK** button to close the window and to return to the Options window.

13 CLICK the **OK** button to close the options window.

Any search that you initiate will now search every file for the topics that contain the words that you type into the first box.

Activity 20.2 Using Find

1 ENSURE that the **Find** dialog box of the Help Topics window is on display.

You will see that there are three boxes that can be used to initiate a search. The first box annotated

Type the word(s) you want to find

is available for you to enter specific words at the keyboard that are pertinent to your search. The second box annotated:

Select some matching words to narrow your search

is available to link with the specific topics listed in the third box that use the words either in their title or in the body of their Help text.

2 USE the slider bar to view the possible words that can be included in a search. You will find that there is a very large number of them.

Searching for a key word amongst this list could take time so:

3 TYPE the key word:

expert

into the first box.

You will see that box 2 contains two selected words expert and Expert. Also box 3 contains just one selected topic:

Tips: Becoming an Expert

4 ENSURE that the topic is selected and CLICK the **Display** button to reveal a Help window containing, amongst other things, a description of the use of the right-hand mouse button:

> **Windows Help**
>
> Help Topics | Back | Options
>
> **Becoming an expert**
>
> - You can use your right mouse button to drag files. Try it and see what happens!
> - You can use long filenames when you save documents. You can even use spaces!
> - You can use your right mouse button to click anywhere and see a menu of available commands.
> - To draw a selection box around a group of files, you can click at a corner of the group, and then drag to form the box.
> - The underlined letters in menus are shortcuts. Press ALT plus the underlined letter to choose the item.
> - You can solve hardware

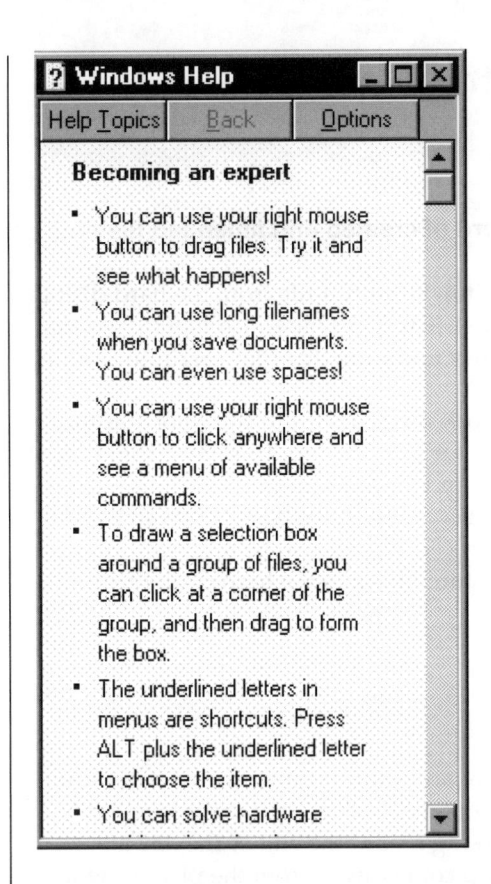

5 CLICK the **Help Topic** button to return to the Find dialog box of the Help window.

6 CLICK the **Clear** button and that search criterion is cleared in readiness for another to be entered.

| Task 21 | # Backing up, restoring and comparing files

➤ **Maintaining a secure record of created and amended files**

We have already demonstrated how to copy a file from the hard disk to a floppy diskette in the external disk drive. We have also mentioned the need to perform this task regularly to ensure that files corrupted on one medium are not irretrievably lost.

Often, at the end of a day's work it is required to copy not just a single file but a whole collection of files for safe storage. To save a single file at a time is tedious and for this reason Windows 95 provides a backup facility whereby a collection of files can be automatically saved to an alternative medium. The same procedure can also be reversed whenever a collection of files have to be restored back to the hard disk. Ensure that the desktop is on display.

Activity 21.1 Backing up files

The whole purpose of taking a backup of files that are resident on your computer's hard disk is to provide a copy of those files on a different medium in a different location to your computer. A company will back up all working files at the end of the day's computing and then (ideally) will take the backup copies away from the place of work overnight. Then, if the following morning the computers have been stolen or damaged in any way the company still has the most recent copy of its valuable files. These files can then be restored back to the hard disk of a new or repaired computer.

The normal media that are used to back up onto are floppy diskettes or a tape streamer, depending upon the number and size of the files that are required to be backed up. To illustrate the process we shall back up the two files that are contained in the Work folder that we created in Activity 18.1.

1   CLICK the **Start** button, SELECT **Progams** and then OPEN the **Accessories** menu.

2   SELECT **System Tools** from the Accessories menu and from the System Tools menu SELECT **Backup**:

- Backup
- Disk Defragmenter
- DriveSpace
- Inbox Repair Tool
- Resource Meter
- ScanDisk

This reveals the Welcome to Microsoft Backup window:

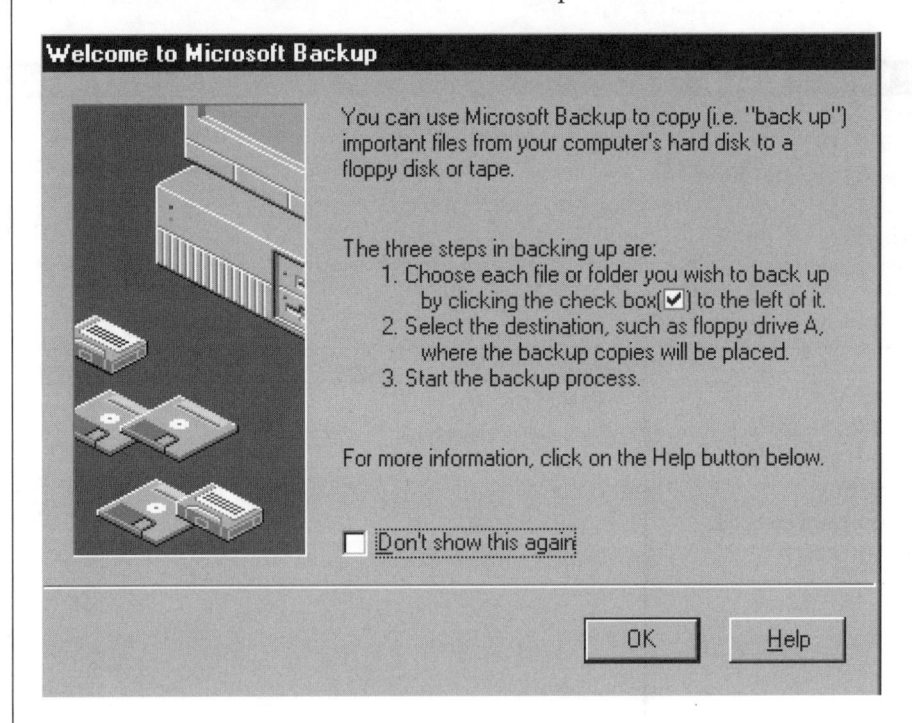

Welcome to Microsoft Backup

You can use Microsoft Backup to copy (i.e. "back up") important files from your computer's hard disk to a floppy disk or tape.

The three steps in backing up are:
1. Choose each file or folder you wish to back up by clicking the check box(☑) to the left of it.
2. Select the destination, such as floppy drive A, where the backup copies will be placed.
3. Start the backup process.

For more information, click on the Help button below.

☐ Don't show this again

[OK]   [Help]

3 READ the contents of this window and if you do not wish the window to appear next time you enter the backup procedure CLICK the check box.

4 CLICK the **OK** button and this window is replaced with a second information window opens informing you that the system has created a Full System Backup file:

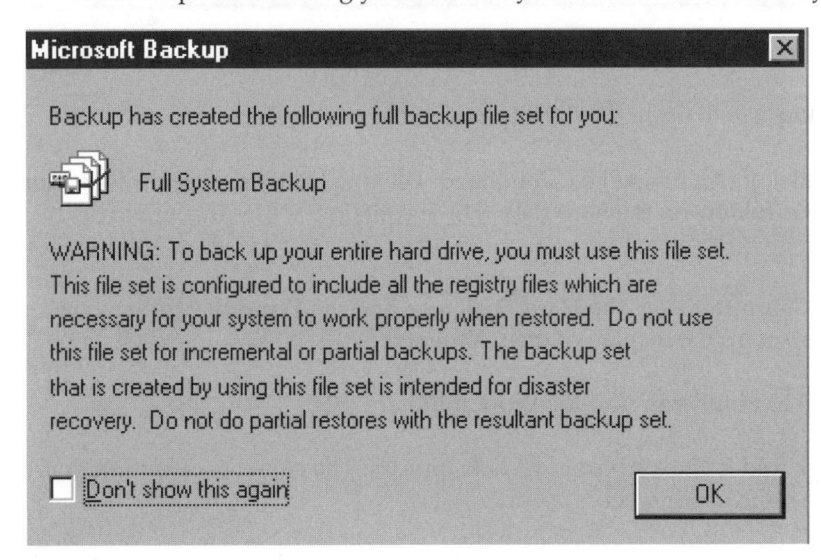

Microsoft Backup

Backup has created the following full backup file set for you:

Full System Backup

WARNING: To back up your entire hard drive, you must use this file set. This file set is configured to include all the registry files which are necessary for your system to work properly when restored. Do not use this file set for incremental or partial backups. The backup set that is created by using this file set is intended for disaster recovery. Do not do partial restores with the resultant backup set.

☐ Don't show this again   [OK]

5 READ this and CLICK the check box if you do not want this to appear the next time that you access this feature.

6 CLICK the **OK** button to close this window and to reveal the Microsoft Backup window:

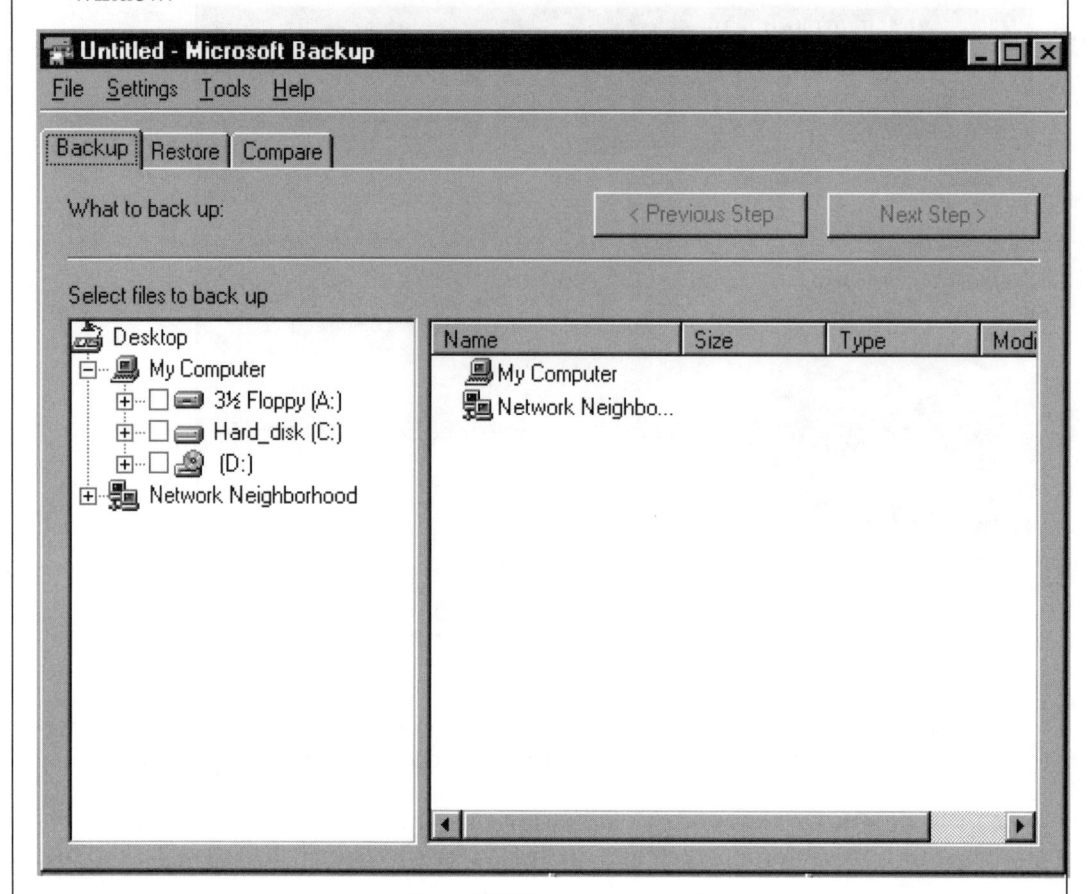

```
┌─────────────────────────────────────────────────────────────────────┐
│ 🖳 Untitled - Microsoft Backup                              _ □ ×   │
│ File  Settings  Tools  Help                                         │
│ ┌────────┐                                                          │
│ │ Backup │ Restore │ Compare │                                      │
│ └────────┘                                                          │
│  What to back up:              [ < Previous Step ]  [ Next Step > ] │
│                                                                     │
│  Select files to back up                                            │
│  ┌──────────────────────────┬────────────────────────────────────┐  │
│  │ 🖳 Desktop               │ Name          Size   Type   Modi   │  │
│  │ ├─ 🖳 My Computer        │ 🖳 My Computer                      │  │
│  │ │  ├─ ☐ 3½ Floppy (A:)   │ 🖳 Network Neighbo...              │  │
│  │ │  ├─ ☐ Hard_disk (C:)   │                                    │  │
│  │ │  └─ ☐ (D:)             │                                    │  │
│  │ └─ 🖳 Network Neighborhood│                                    │  │
│  │                          │                                    │  │
│  └──────────────────────────┴────────────────────────────────────┘  │
└─────────────────────────────────────────────────────────────────────┘
```

There are three dialog boxes in this window.

7 CLICK the **Backup** tab to bring the Backup dialog box to the fore.

In the left-hand panel of this dialog box, annotated 'What to back up:', are the icons and names of the various folders on the hard disk. These contain the files that are to be backed up.

8 CLICK the **My Computer** icon, the **Hard Disk** icon and the **Windows folder** icon check boxes to open up the display of their contents.

9 CLICK the scroll bar until you find the Work folder.

10 CLICK the **Work** folder chexck box and a tick appears. The contents of the folder are displayed in the right-hand panel.

We wish to back up the contents of the Work folder to a floppy diskette in the external drive.

11 PLACE a formatted floppy diskette in the external drive (*Refer* to Activity 18.2: Formatting a floppy diskette).

12 CLICK the **Next Step** button.

The left-hand panel is now annotated Where to back up: and it displays the icon of the external drive, the $3^1/_2$ Floppy (A:\) icon.

13 CLICK the **$3^1/_2$ Floppy (A:\)** icon and in the right-hand panel in the Selected device or location box the target A:\ appears.

14 CLICK the **Start Backup** button and the Backup Set Label window appears.

When a collection of files are backed up they are not saved onto the backup medium as a collection of single files. Rather they are saved collectively as a single file and it is here that we must give that file a name.

15 ENTER the name:

Work

into the Backup set box.

Notice that there is an option to attach a password to this backup file so that unauthorized individuals can be excluded from viewing the contents.

16 CLICK the **OK** button.

A Backup window appears that shows the progress of the backup as it proceeds. Eventually, an information window appears informing you that the operation is complete.

17 CLICK the **OK** button in the information window and then CLICK the **OK** button in the Backup window and you are returned to the display of the Microsoft Backup window.

The backing up is now complete but do not close down the Microsoft Backup window as we shall start from here in the next *Activity*. For the same reason leave the floppy diskette in the external drive

Activity 21.2 Restoring files

Having found out how to intiate the backup procedure we must now learn how to reverse the procedure and restore backup files back to the hard disk.

1 ENSURE that the Microsoft Backup window is on display and that the floppy diskette containing the backup files is inside the external drive.

2 CLICK the **Restore** tab to bring the Restore dialog box to the fore:

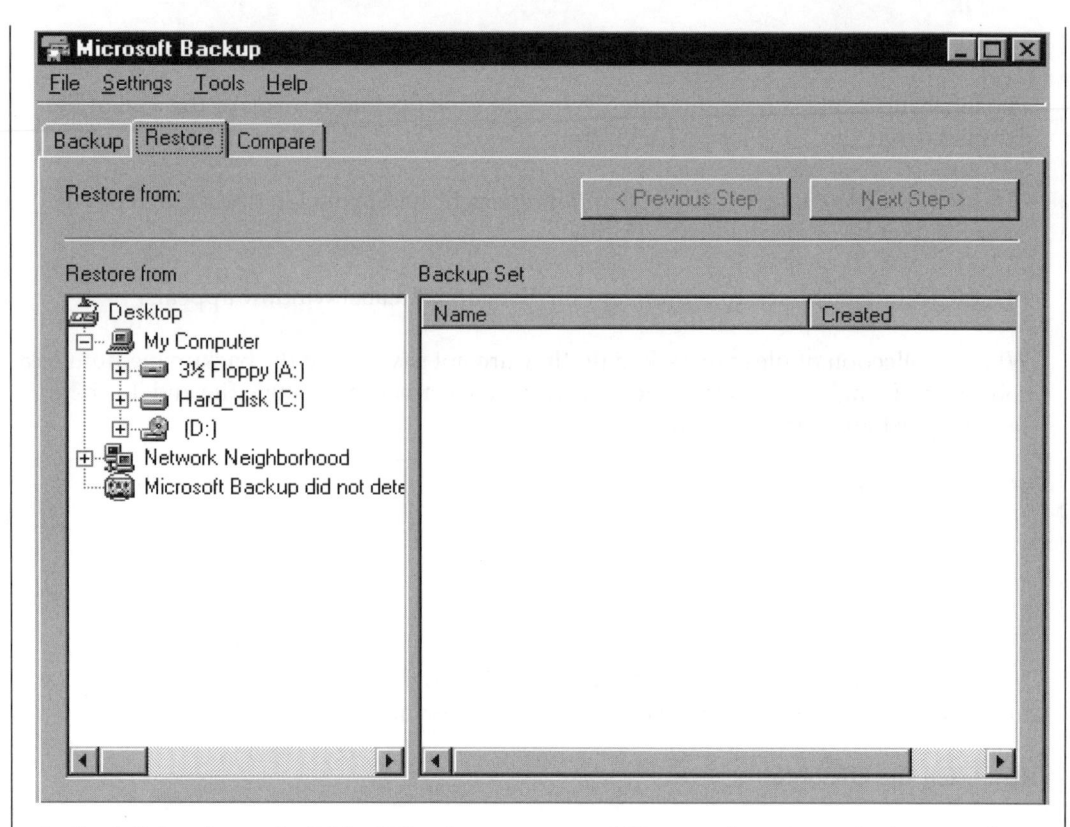

[Screenshot of Microsoft Backup window showing the Restore tab with a 'Restore from:' tree panel listing Desktop, My Computer, 3½ Floppy (A:), Hard_disk (C:), (D:), Network Neighborhood, and a Backup Set panel with Name and Created columns.]

In the left-hand panel of this dialog box, annotated 'Restore from:', are the icons and names of the various folders that might contain the files to be restored. To avoid any problems that may occur when overwriting files that already exist on the hard disk we shall have to amend one of the Restore settings.

3 CLICK the **Settings** command on the Menu bar to reveal a drop-down menu of further options:

[Screenshot of Settings drop-down menu showing File Filtering..., Drag and Drop..., Options...]

4 SELECT **Options** to reveal the Setting-Options window containing four dialog boxes.

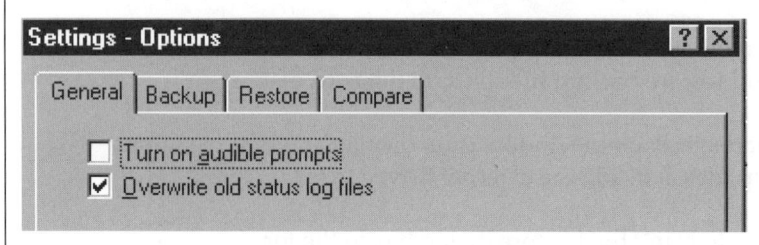

[Screenshot of Settings - Options dialog with tabs General, Backup, Restore, Compare. General tab shows unchecked 'Turn on audible prompts' and checked 'Overwrite old status log files'.]

5 CLICK the **Restore** tab to bring the Restore dialog box to the fore and CLICK the bottom radio button annotated Overwrite files in the Advanced Options box.

6 CLICK the **OK** button to close this window and to return to the Restore dialog box of the Microsoft Backup window.

7 CLICK the **3^1/$_2$ Floppy (A:\)** icon and the backupfile appears in the right-hand panel.

8 CLICK the **Next Step** button and in the right-hand panel, annotated

   Contents of "Work.QIC"

   is an icon labelled C:

9 CLICK the check box of the icon in the right-hand panel and a tick appears.

Ticks also appear in the left-hand panel indicating the path the restored file will take.

10 CLICK the **Start Restore** button and a Restore window opens informing you of the progress of the procedure.

11 When the restore is complete CLICK the **OK** button in the Restore window to return you to the Microsoft Backup window.

All appears in order but as a final check we need to compare the restored file on the hard disk with the original file on the floppy disk.

Activity 21.3 **Comparing files**

1 ENSURE that the Microsoft Backup window is on display and that the floppy diskette used to restore the Work folder is in the external drive.

2 CLICK the **Settings** command on the menu bar and SELECT **Options...** to reveal the Settings - Options window:

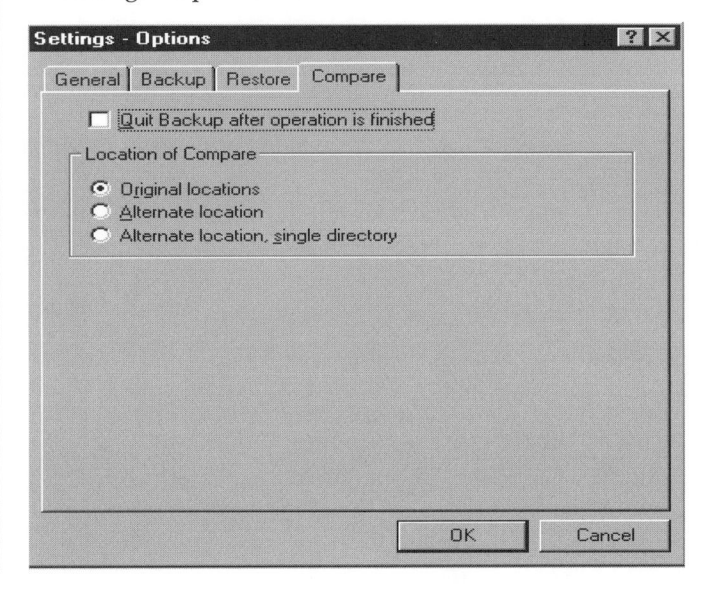

Backing up, restoring and comparing files 97

3   CLICK the **Compare** tab to bring the Compare dialog box to the fore.

4   ENSURE the Options are as displayed.

5   CLICK the **OK** button to close the Settings - Options window.

6   CLICK the **3$^{1}/_{2}$ Floppy (A:)** icon in the Compare from panel to open the contents in the right-hand panel.

7   CLICK the **Work.QIC** icon in the Backup set panel on the right-hand side.

8   CLICK the **Next Step** button.

9   In the **Files to compare** window SELECT files from the backup set in the left-hand panel by clicking the Windows check box.

10 CLICK the **Start Compare** button and a Compare window opens to indicate the progress of the comparison.

Eventually an information window opens indicating that the operation is complete.

11 CLICK the **OK** button in the information window and then CLICK the **OK** button in the Compare window.

Because no message was produced the two files have been successfully compared and found to be identical.

Section D

Advanced features

By now, manipulating the Windows 95 GUI environment will be almost second nature. Like riding your bike, you will be well balanced and taking more care of where you are going rather than how you are going to get there. There may, however, still be one or two features that you have not quite settled into; perhaps you dislike the screen colours, maybe the mouse needs some adjustment. In this Section you will learn how to fine tune the 'feel' of the Windows 95 system to suit your personal desires.

By accessing the facilities offered in the Control Panel you will learn how to:

- change the various features of the display and data input to suit your personal preferences
- protect your files by installing a password on the screen saver
- adapt the system to cater for disabled users
- install an application package

Task 22: Customizing the display
Task 23: Password protection
Task 24: Keyboard and mouse settings
Task 25: Accessibility options
Task 26: Installing Microsoft Excel 5.0

| Task 22 | # Customizing the display

> **Changing the colours, text style and overall appearance of the screen**

Ensure that the desktop is on display.

Activity 22.1 **Changing the desktop background display**

1 DOUBLE-CLICK the **My Computer** icon to open the My Computer window:

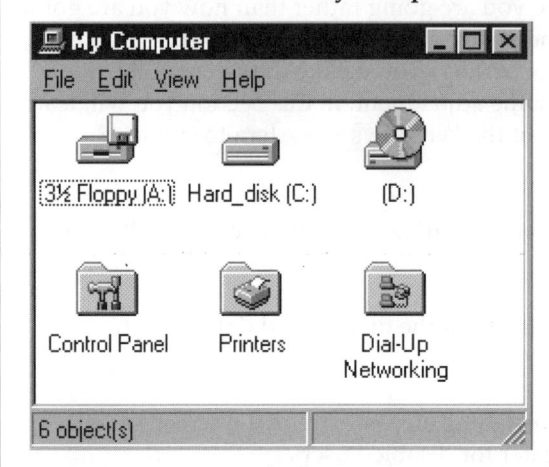

```
My Computer
File  Edit  View  Help

  3½ Floppy (A:)   Hard_disk (C:)   (D:)

  Control Panel   Printers   Dial-Up Networking

6 object(s)
```

2 DOUBLE-CLICK the **Control Panel** icon to open the Control Panel window:

```
Control Panel
File  Edit  View  Help

Accessibility   Add New      Add/Remove   Date/Time   Display
Options         Hardware     Programs

Fonts           Joystick     Keyboard     Mail and Fax  Microsoft Mail
                                                        Postoffice

Modems          Mouse        Multimedia   Network      Passwords

Printers        Regional     Sounds       System
```

3 DOUBLE-CLICK the **Display** icon to open the Display Properties window

100 Advanced features

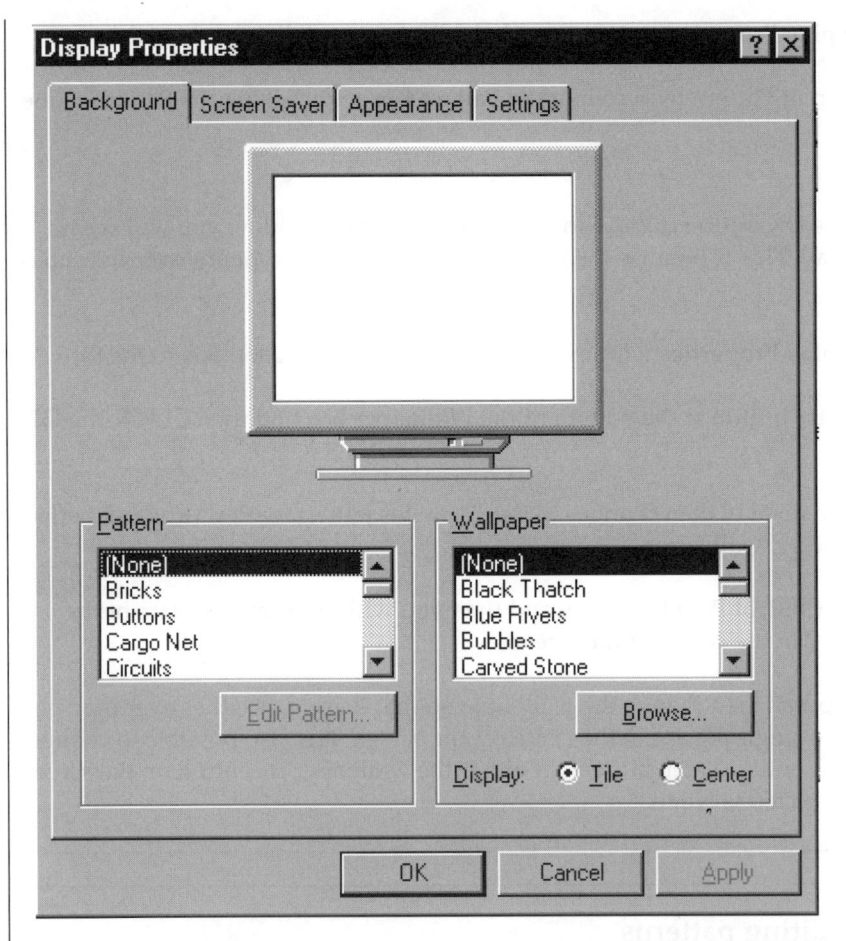

The Display Properties window contains four dialog boxes, each with its own tab.

4 CLICK the **Background** tab to bring the Background dialog box to the fore.

The Background box permits changes to the desktop display to be made. The display consists of two aspects, Pattern and Wallpaper.

5 USE the scroll bars at either side of the Pattern and Wallpaper boxes to view the names of all the possibilities that are available.

A different Wallpaper is selected by scrolling the Wallpaper box and clicking the wallpaper name. To view the effect of each wallpaper click the Tile button and the simulated computer screen in the top of the window changes to reflect your choice.

6 CLICK the **OK** button to see the actual effect on the desktop.

7 CHANGE the **Wallpaper** to Bubbles, CLICK the **Tile** button and then CLICK the **OK** button to view the effect on the desktop display.

The display window has closed and the desktop background has changed to the wallpaper that has been selected. To change the wallpaper again you will have to re-open the Display Properties window from the Control Panel window.

8 OPEN the **Display Properties** window with the Background dialog box to the fore.

9 SELECT a different Pattern by scrolling the Pattern box and clicking the Pattern name:

Triangles

When you click the OK button to close the Display Properties window you will see no effect on the display. This is because the tiled wallpaper takes precedence over the choice of pattern.

10 OPEN the **Display Properties** window with the Background dialog box to the fore.

11 CLICK the **Centre** button at the bottom of the Wallpaper box and then CLICK the **OK** button.

The desktop screen display then changes to the Triangles pattern with no apparent effect caused by the choice of wallpaper.

12 MINIMIZE the **Control Panel** window and then you will see a small square of the Bubbles wallpaer in the centre of the screen.

In summary, it is possible to change the wallpaper so that it appears either over the entire screen or as a single square in the centre of the screen. It is also possible to change the pattern over the entire screen but only if either the wallpaper is centred on the screen or the wallpaper selected is None.

Activity 22.2 Editing patterns

It is possible to create your own pattern.

1 ENSURE that the **Display Properties** window is on display with the Background dialog box to the fore.

2 ENSURE that the Wallpaper selected is None

3 SELECT any pattern and CLICK the **Edit Pattern** button to reveal the Edit Pattern window:

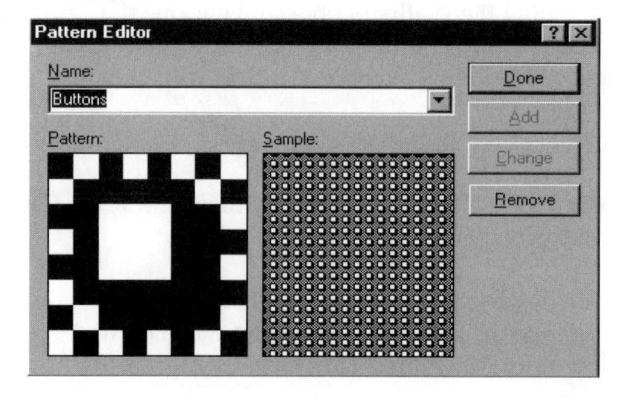

The small square to the left shows the detailed pattern comprising small dark and light squares that is repeated to produce the overall pattern shown in the right-hand square. The pattern on the left can be amended by clicking each of the small squares. Each time a small square is clicked it changes from light to dark or vice versa.

4   CHANGE the pattern of small squares to look like the following:

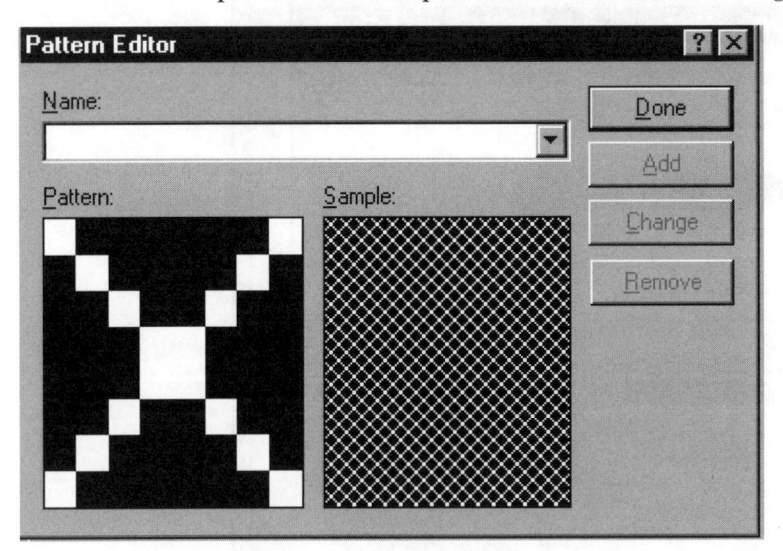

The effect on the screen is given in the right-hand square:

5 GIVE this pattern the name:

   Diagonals

6 CLICK the **Add** button and this adds this pattern to the list.

7 CLICK the **Done** button and then CLICK the **OK** button and the desktop display is amended accordingly.

Activity 22.3 Changing the appearance of screen items

1 ENSURE that the Display Properties window is on display.

2 CLICK the **Appearance** tab to bring the Appearance dialog box to the fore:

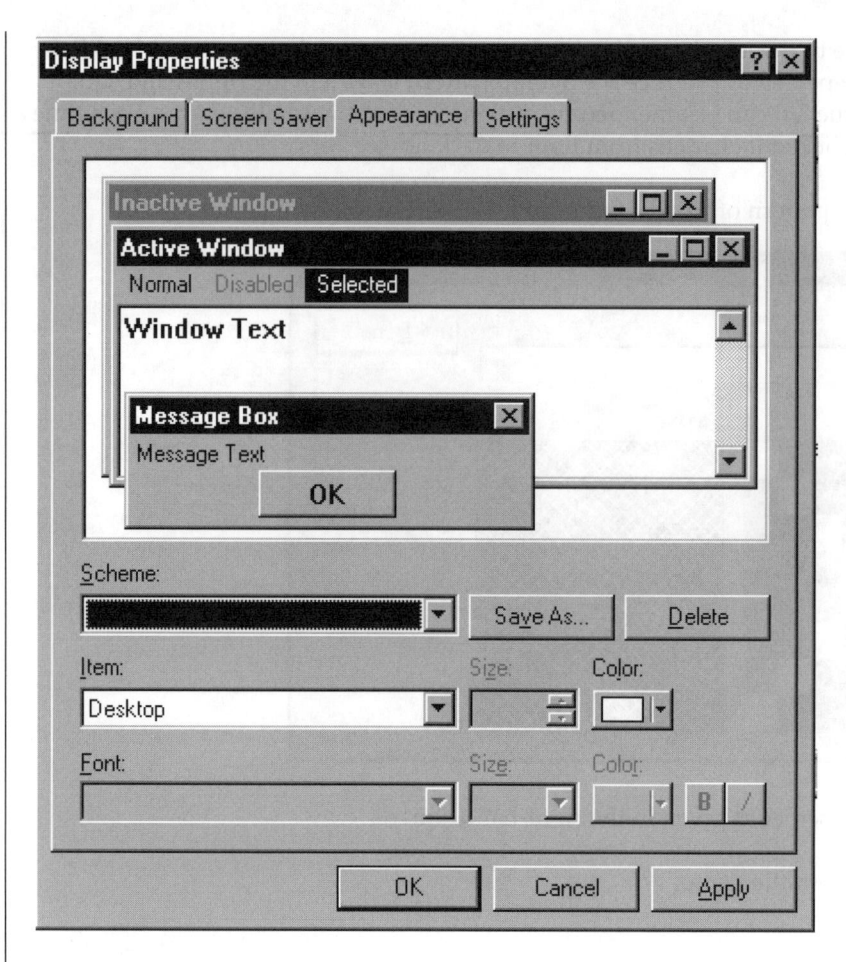

The top half of this dialog box displays the various features whose appearance can be amended. Below this display is a box annotated as Scheme.

3   CLICK the **Scheme** list box arrow to reveal a list of different colour schemes:

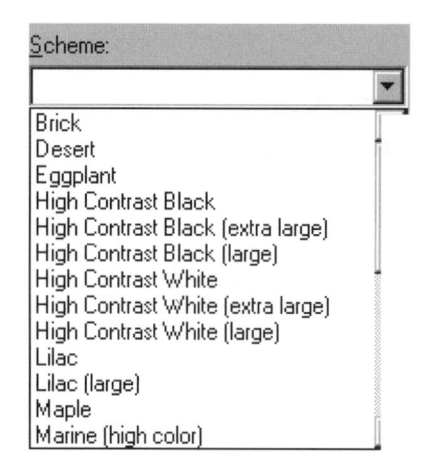

4   SELECT each scheme in turn to see the effect on the display in the upper half of the dialog box.

Notice that the default scheme has no name. If none of these schemes meet with your approval then it is possible to devise your own.

5 CLICK the **Item** list box arrow to reveal a list of items:

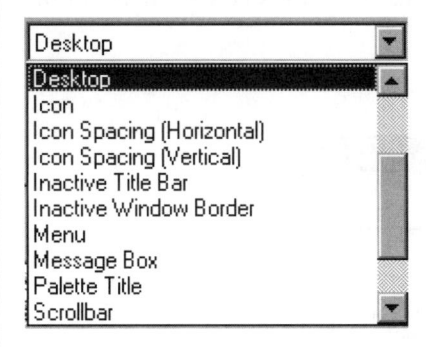

```
Desktop
Desktop
Icon
Icon Spacing (Horizontal)
Icon Spacing (Vertical)
Inactive Title Bar
Inactive Window Border
Menu
Message Box
Palette Title
Scrollbar
```

Each of these items can be given a chosen colour by selecting from the Colour list box to the immediate right of the Item list box.

6 SELECT the **Desktop** from the Item list box and then SELECT bright red from the Colour list box.

The desktop display at the top of the dialog box changes to dark red.

7 CLICK the **OK** button to see the effect on the actual desktop.

8 RE-OPEN the **Display Properties** window with the Appearance dialog box to the fore.

If the Item selected from the Item list box is text then it becomes possible to change the size, font, colour and style of the text.

9 SELECT **Menu** from the Item list box.

The item selected is the menu bar that appears in an active window.

10 CHANGE the **Size** from 18 to 24 by clicking the size arrows at the side of the Size box:

```
Menu                      24
```

This changes the size of the menu bar.

11 SELECT the **Colour** to be bright yellow.

The colour change is reflected in the display in the top half of the dialog box.

12 From the Font list box SELECT the font **Courier**, CHANGE the **Size** (of font) to 15, SELECT the COLOUR to be bright red.

The style of the font can also be changed.

13 CLICK the **B** button (for bold font) and the **I** button (for italics) and view the effect.

Next we want to save this setting as a new scheme.

14 CLICK the **Save As...** button and in the Save As... dialog box ENTER the name of the scheme as:

Flaming daffodil

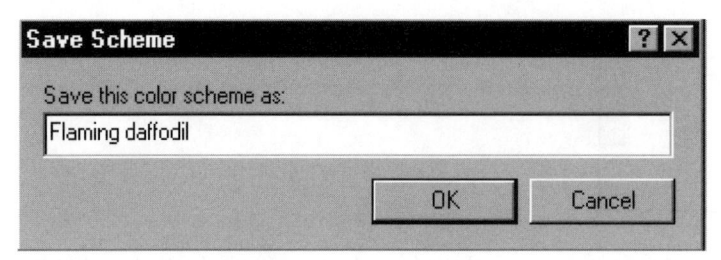

and CLICK the **OK** button.

This saves the scheme to disk. Next we need to apply the scheme.

15 CLICK the **Apply** button followed by the **OK** button and the new scheme is applied.

Do not worry if you do not like the effect.

16 RETURN to the **Display Properties** window and re-apply the default scheme – it is the one with no name.

Activity 22.4 Changing the Settings

1 ENSURE that the **Display Properties** window is open.

2 CLICK the **Settings** tab to reveal the Settings dialog box:

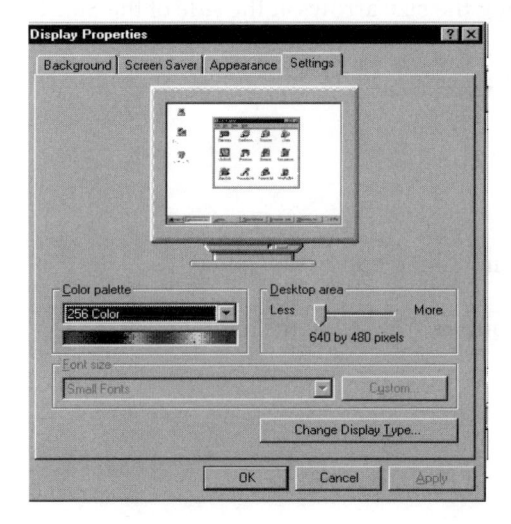

The purpose of this dialog box is to permit you to cater for different monitors and adaptor cards – the adaptor card is a piece of hardware that fits inside your computer and controls the display that you see on the monitor.

3   CLICK the **Change Display Type** to reveal the Display Type dialog box:

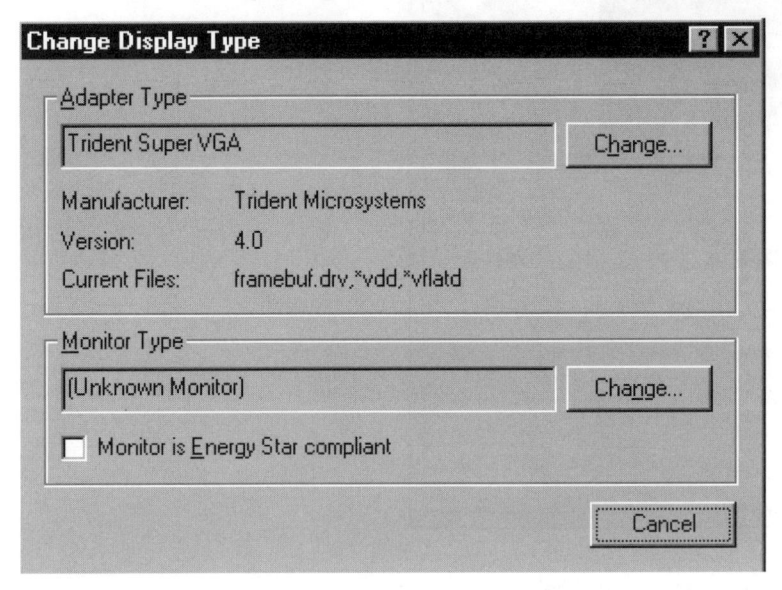

```
Change Display Type                                    ? X
┌─Adapter Type─────────────────────────────────────┐
│  Trident Super VGA                    Change...  │
│                                                  │
│  Manufacturer:    Trident Microsystems           │
│  Version:         4.0                            │
│  Current Files:   framebuf.drv,*vdd,*vflatd      │
└──────────────────────────────────────────────────┘
┌─Monitor Type─────────────────────────────────────┐
│  (Unknown Monitor)                    Change...  │
│                                                  │
│  ☐ Monitor is Energy Star compliant              │
└──────────────────────────────────────────────────┘
                                         Cancel
```

By using the scroll bars at the sides of the Adapter Type and Monitor boxes you can cater for the installation of any one of a number of options. The types of adaptor and monitor will control the limits to which you can change the eventual screen display.

4   CLOSE the **Change Display Type** dialog box and return to the Settings dialog box.

The Colour palette permits a display of either 16 or 256 colours and which applies depends upon your adaptor and monitor. Font sizes can be selected to be either Small or Large. It is also possible to customize the font size.

5   CLICK the **Custom** button to reveal the Custom Font Size window.

6   DRAG the ruler to see the effect on the displayed font

Activity 22.5 Changing the screen saver

If a computer is left on with a static display the bright parts of the display can, over time, leave a permanent mark on the interior of the display screen. To lessen the chances of this happening screen savers are available; a screen saver is a non-static display with a reduced amount of screen usage overall.

1   ENSURE that the **Display Properties** window is on view.

2   CLICK the **Screen Saver** tab to bring the Screen Saver dialog box to the fore:

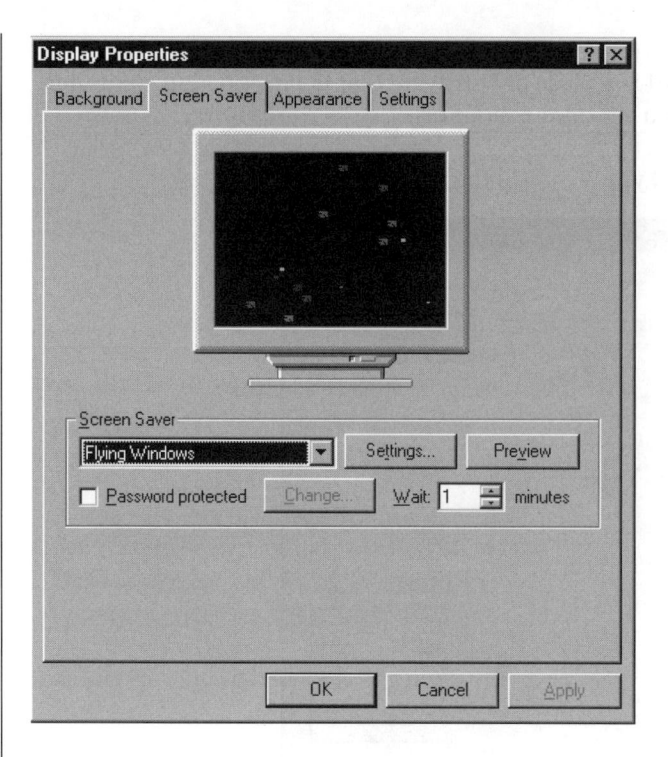

3 OPEN the **Screen Saver** list box and select each name in turn.

You will see the effect simulated on the display panel in the top half of the dialog box.

4 To see how the effect actually looks CLICK the **Preview** button. CLICK the mouse button at any time to return to the Screen Saver dialog box.

5 CLICK the **Settings...** button to open the Settings dialog box:

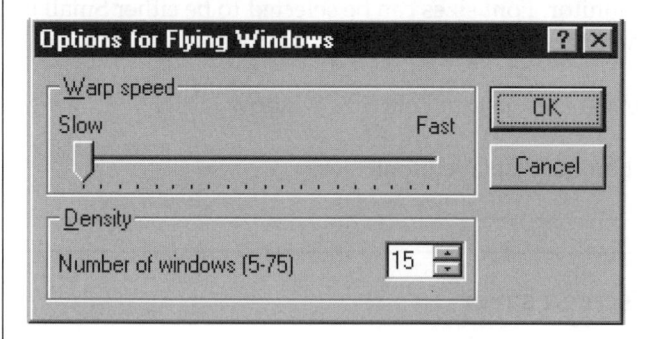

6 VIEW the effects of changing the Warp Speed and Density values.

7 When you have the desired speed and density CLICK the **OK** button.

The Wait box refers to the number of minutes to elapse between the computer standing idle and the screen saver switching into operation.

Task 23 — Password protection

➤ **Installing a password to prevent unauthorized access**
Ensure that the desktop is on display

Activity 23.1 Windows 95 Password protection

Passwords are used to prevent unauthorized access to your computer. We shall assume that no password has been set up for access to Windows 95 and that you wish one to be installed.

1 DISPLAY the **Control Panel** window and locate the Passwords icon:

Passwords

2 DOUBLE-CLICK the **Passwords** icon to reveal the Passwords Properties window:

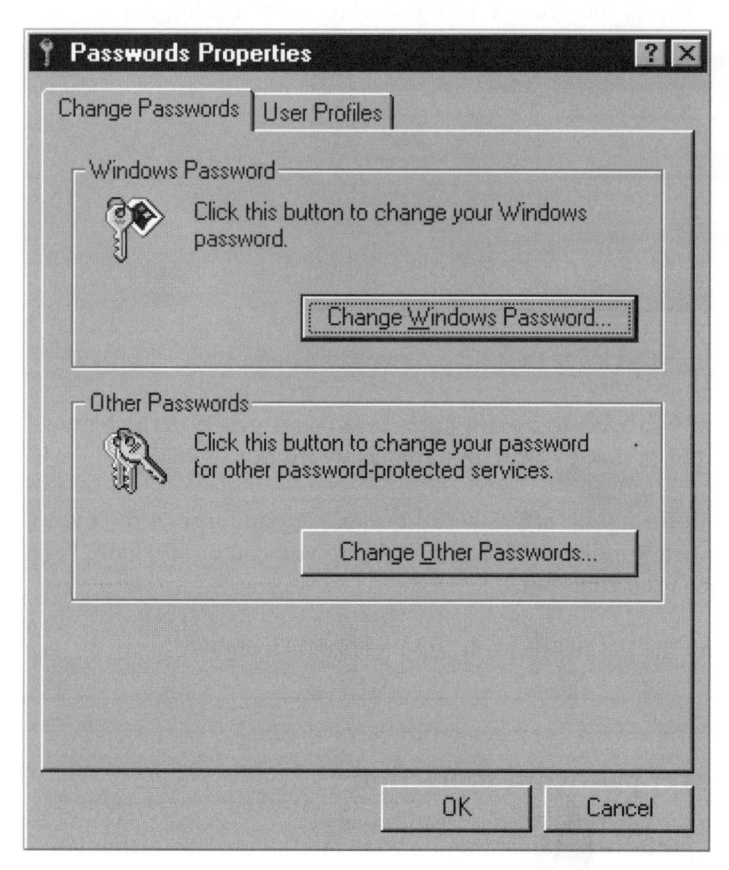

```
Passwords Properties                              ? X
┌─────────────────────────────────────────────────┐
│ Change Passwords │ User Profiles │              │
│                                                 │
│  ┌─ Windows Password ──────────────────────┐    │
│  │                                         │    │
│  │   Click this button to change your      │    │
│  │   Windows password.                     │    │
│  │                                         │    │
│  │         [ Change Windows Password... ]  │    │
│  └─────────────────────────────────────────┘    │
│                                                 │
│  ┌─ Other Passwords ───────────────────────┐    │
│  │                                         │    │
│  │   Click this button to change your      │    │
│  │   password for other password-protected │    │
│  │   services.                             │    │
│  │                                         │    │
│  │         [ Change Other Passwords... ]   │    │
│  └─────────────────────────────────────────┘    │
│                                                 │
│              [   OK   ]   [ Cancel ]            │
└─────────────────────────────────────────────────┘
```

3 In the box annotated Windows Password CLICK the **Change Windows Password** button to reveal the Change Windows Password information window:

Change Windows Password

You may also change other passwords at the same time as your Windows password.

Check the other passwords you would like to change to use the same password as your Windows password.

☐ Windows Screen Saver

[OK]   [Cancel]

Not only can you change or install your Windows password but you can also install a Windows screen saver password. We shall not do this at the moment.

4 CLICK the **OK** button to reveal the Change Windows Password Dialog box:

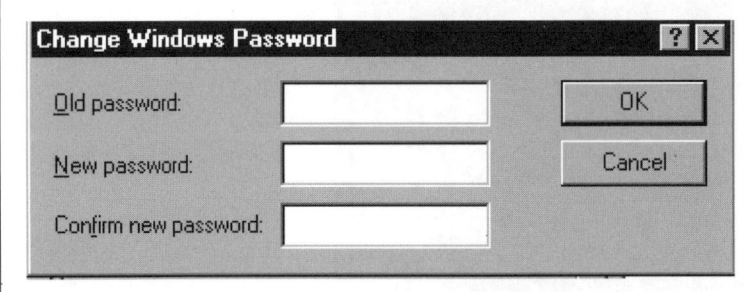

Change Windows Password

Old password: [   ]   [OK]
New password: [   ]   [Cancel]
Confirm new password: [   ]

The old password does not exist so leave the Old password box empty.

5 ENTER the password that you wish to use for entry into Windows 95 in the **New password** box. REPEAT this is in the **Confirm new password** box.

Beware: Take great care about the choice of password because if you forget it then you will have to re-install the entire Windows 95 program before you can use it again. For the purposes of this book use your first name.

6 CLICK the **OK** button and the password protection feature is installed.

Activity 23.2 **Screen Saver password protection**

Even though you have now protected against unauthorized password protection you will not have eliminated unauthorized access completely. If you leave your computer for any reason without leaving Windows first anyone else can take your place. To eliminate this problem and obviate the requirement of leaving Windows every time you leave your computer we shall put a password protection on the Screen Saver.

1 OPEN the **Control Panel** window and DOUBLE-CLICK the **Display** icon to reveal the Display Properties window.

2 CLICK the **Screen Saver** tab to bring the Screen Saver dialog box to the fore.

3 CLICK the **Password** protected check box to ensure that it contains a tick.

4 CLICK the **Change** button to reveal the Change Password dialog box.

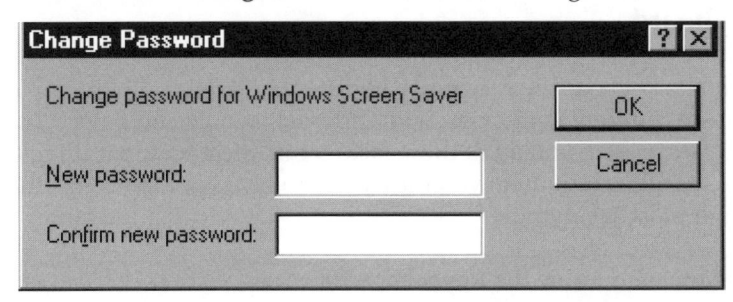

5 ENTER the password (your first name) in the New and Confirm new password boxes and then CLICK the **OK** button.

An information window will appear telling you that the password has been successfully installed.

6 CLICK the **OK** button to close this window.

Now, when ever you try to interrupt the Screen Saver to continue working with your files a dialog box will appear asking you to enter your password:

Password protection 111

| Task 24 | # Keyboard and mouse settings

➤ **Customizing the keyboard and mouse operation.**

Ensure that the desktop is on display

Activity 24.1 The keyboard

Whilst you may think that one keyboard is very much like another that is only true up to a point. Keyboards operate in different languages, with different layouts and have different response rates to key presses and all of these factors can affect your handling of the keyboard. Fortunately, Windows 95 offers you the chance to give your keyboard that operating feel that tyou find most satisfying.

1   DISPLAY the **Control Panel** and locate the Keyboard icon:

Keyboard

2   DOUBLE-CLICK the **Keyboard** icon to reveal the Keyboard Properties window:

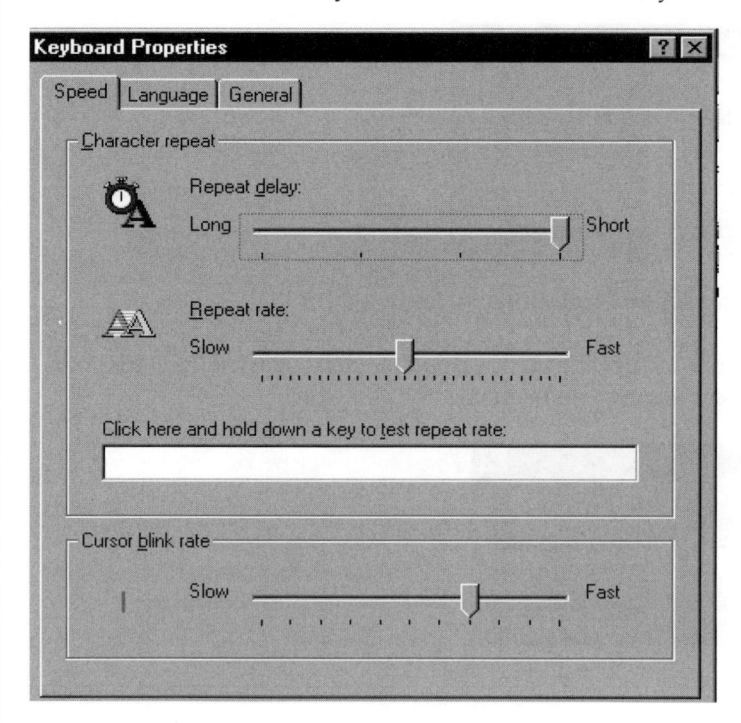

3   CLICK the **Speed** tab to bring the Speed dialog box to the fore.

There are two boxes in this dialog box; Character repeat and Cursor blink rate.

Repeat delay
This scale adjusts the time delay between holding a key down and the repeated character appearing on the screen. If you have a tendency to hold keys down when you type then a longer time delay is required than if you are a quick key tapper.

Repeat rate
This scale adjusts the rate at which a repeated character repeats itself on the screen when a key is held down. Again, if you are a fast typist then this rate can be set higher than if you are a slow typist.

Cursor blink rate
Cursors have a property of being easily lost from view. The rate at which a cursor blinks, coupled with your visual reponse rate, are directly related to the ease with which you can detect the cursor.

4   SET these three scales at a level to suit your personal preferences.

5   CLICK the **Language** tab to bring the Language dialog box to the fore:

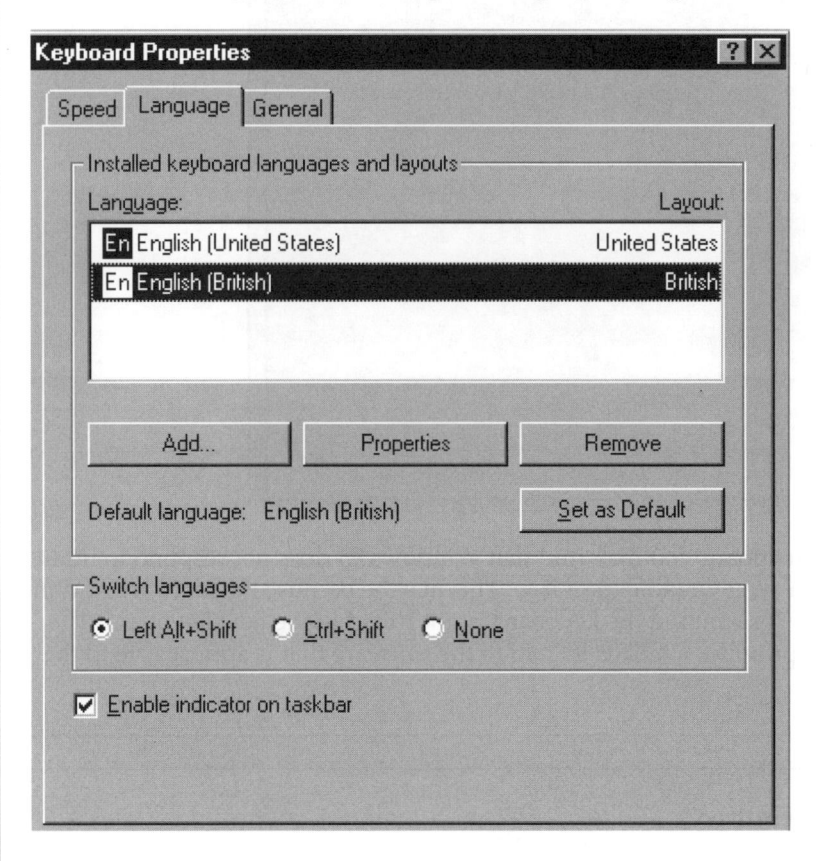

A French keyboard differs from an English keyboard by the inclusion of certain accented characters. A Greek keyboard has a character set that is completely different from either. Also within a given language there may be more than one key layout. This dialog box allows you to defined both the default language and the default keyboard layout. If you wish to use more than one language during your use of windows then you can load another language into memory when you first enter Windows and by pressing either the **Alt-Shift** key combination or the **Ctrl-Shift** combination whilst operating within Windows 95 you can automatically switch from one language to another – that is one character set to another. We shall not perform this operation here as it will require that you have access to the Windows 95 setup disks.

6   CLICK the **General** tab to bring the General dialog box to the fore:

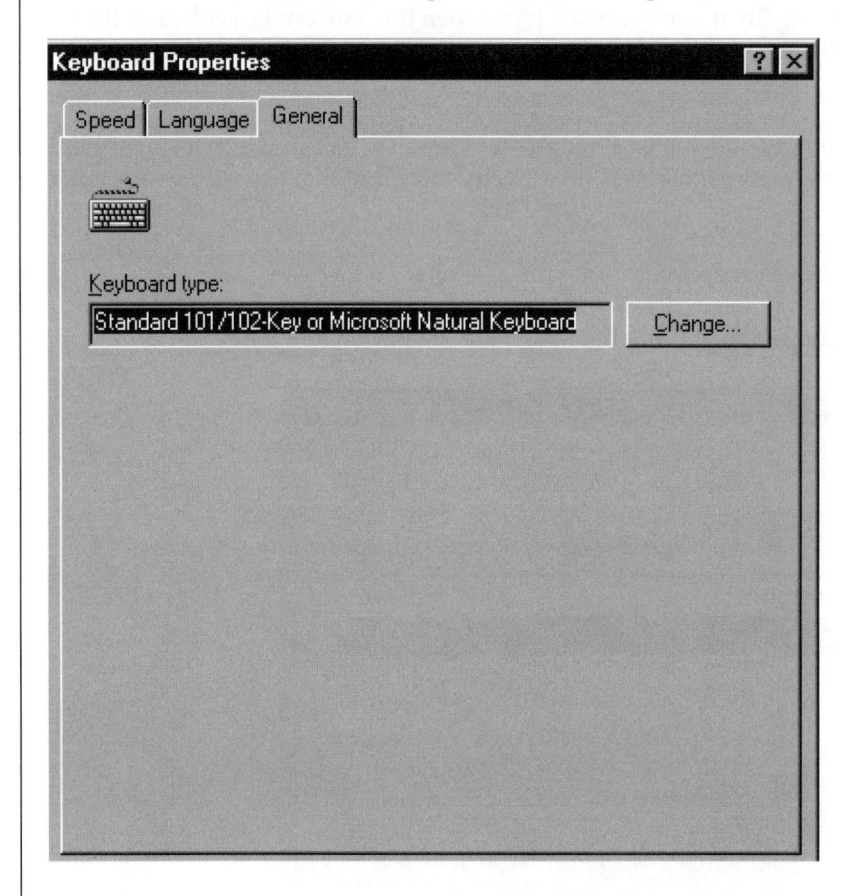

If you instll a new keyboard you may find that Windows 95 does not respond to input from the keyboard as you would expect it to. This may be because the software in Windows 95 responsible for running the keyboard is not suited to the new keyboard. The General dialog box provides a means to load in the software that is appropriate to the new keyboard.

Activity 24.2 The mouse

Just as every keyboard can have its own idiosyncracies so can each mouse.

1   From the Control Panel window DOUBLE-CLICK the **Mouse** icon to reveal the Mouse Properties window:

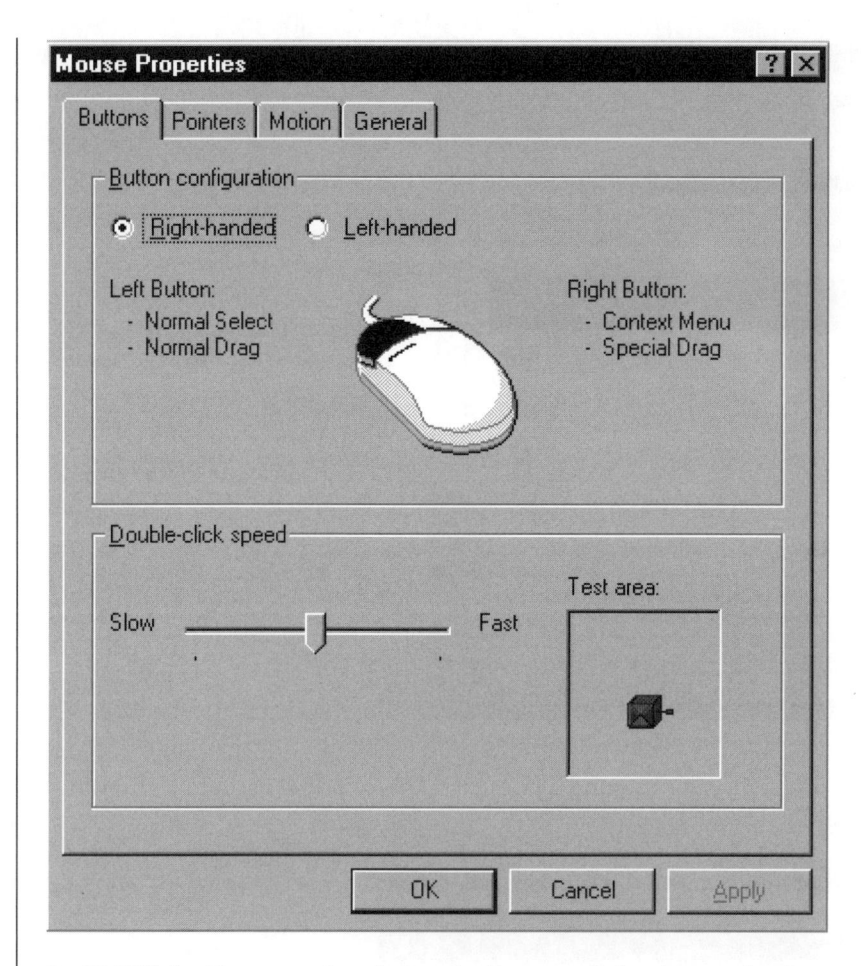

2 CLICK the **Buttons** tab to bring the Buttons dialog box to the fore.

Here you see that you can set the mouse to be either left- or right-handed as well as setting the double-click speed.

3 SET the mouse for your handedness and set the double-click speed to reflect your manual dexterity.

When you change the double-click speed you can test the effect in the test area – try it:

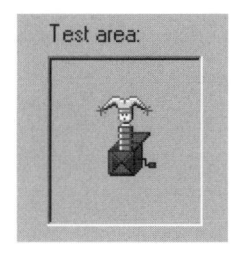

4 CLICK the **Pointer** tab to reveal the Pointers dialog box:

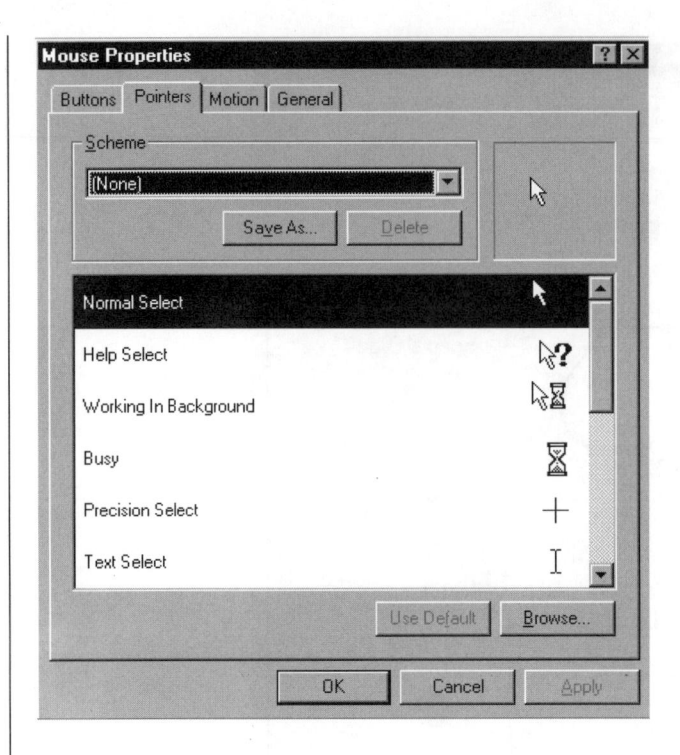

There is very little possibility of changing a pointer in this window except by choosing Animated Hourglass.

5 CLICK the **Motion** tab to reveal the Motion dialog box:

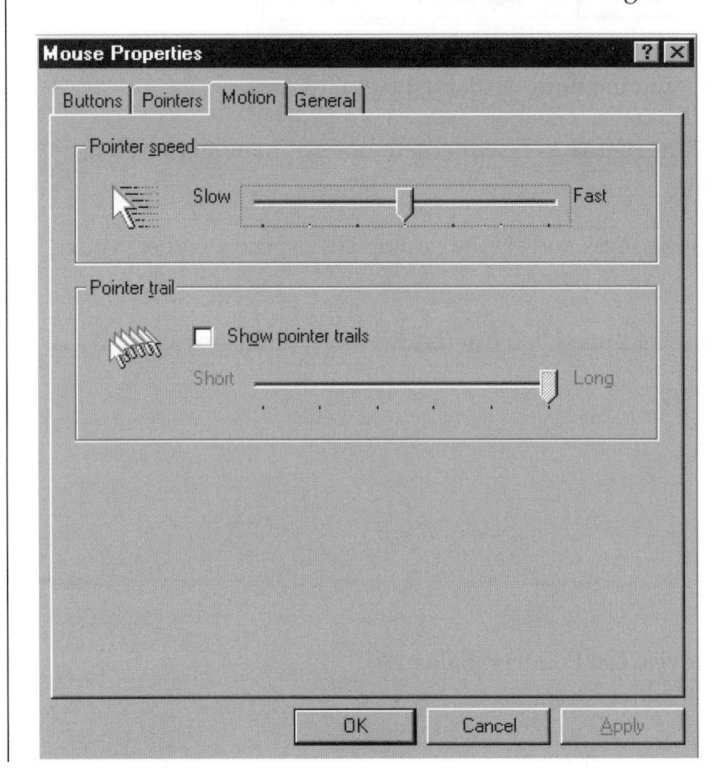

There are two adjustments possible via this window:

Pointer speed
This relates to the speed with which the pointer moves across the screen in relation to the speed and distance the mouse move across the workbench.

Pointer trail
This permits the pointer to leave a trail as it moves across the screen.

6 SET both of these scales to suit your personal preferences.

7 CLICK the **General** tab to reveal the General dialog box.

As with the keyboard this lets you install a different mouse by providing a means to load in the software appropriate to the new mouse.

Activity 24.3 Regional settings

1 DOUBLE-CLICK the **Regional Settings** icon in the Control Panel to reveal the Regional Settings window:

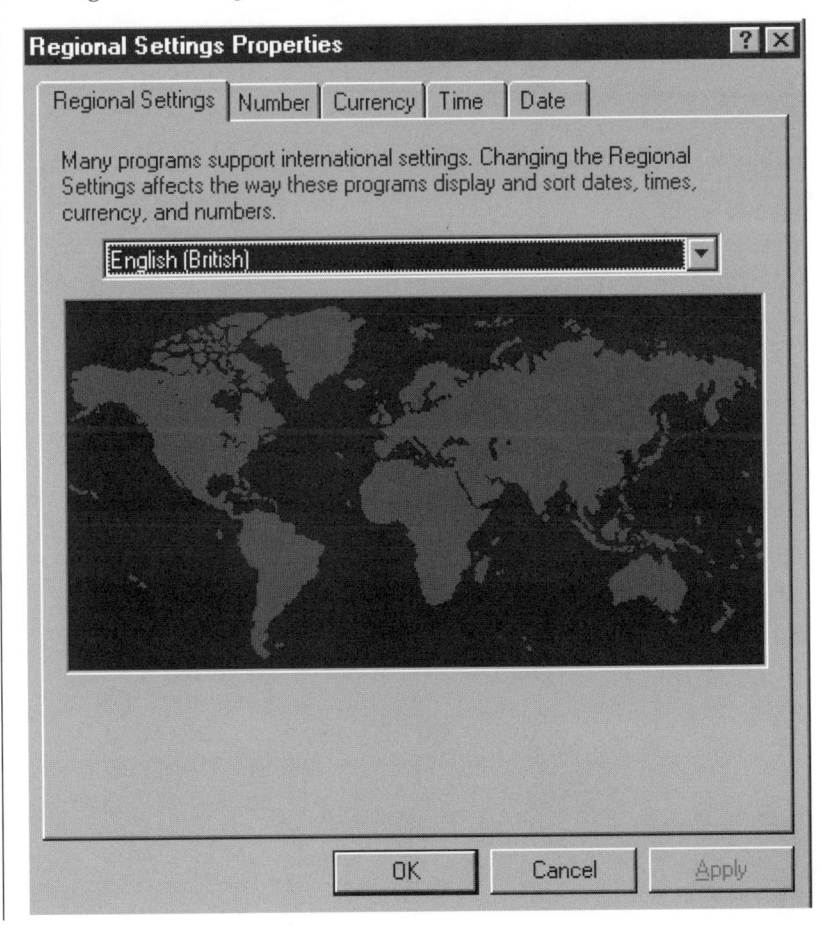

There are four dialog boxes in this window, each one dealing with some aspect of the computer's display that may change from one part of the world to another.

2   CLICK the **Regional Settings** list box arrow to view the number of different settings that are possible.

3   USE the list box to ensure that this is English (British).

Selecting this setting automatically sets the way number, currency, time and date are displayed. However, it is possible to amend these latter displays by way of the appropriate dialog boxes in this window.

4   CLICK the **Number**, **Currency**, **Time** and **Date** tabs in turn to view the settings.

| Task 25 | # Accessibility options

➤ **Options that are available within Windows 95 to cater for users with disabilities**

Ensure that the desktop is on display.

Windows 95 recognizes that not everyone can use a keyboard or mouse with equal dexterity, not everyone can see or hear with equal acuity and that some people have very special needs when it comes to entering information into the computer.

Activity 25.1 Keyboard

1 OPEN the **Control Panel** window and locate the Accessibility Options icon:

[Accessibility Options icon]

2 DOUBLE-CLICK the **Accessibility Options** icon to reveal the Accessibility Properties window:

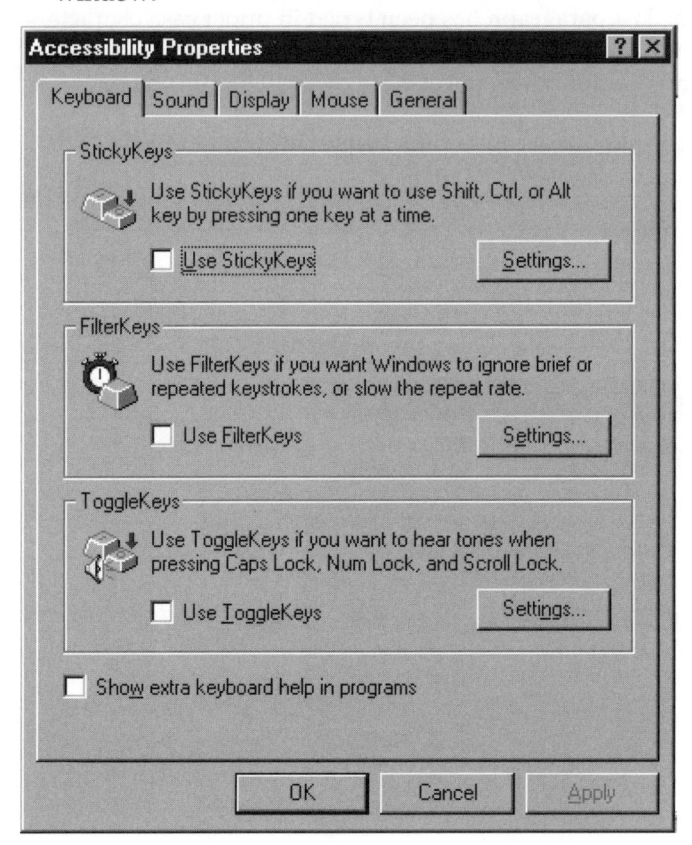

[Accessibility Properties dialog showing Keyboard tab with StickyKeys, FilterKeys, and ToggleKeys sections, and a "Show extra keyboard help in programs" checkbox, with OK, Cancel, and Apply buttons]

There are five dialog boxes available from this window, each one of them offering adjustments and setting changes to the system designed to aid users with particular operating difficulties.

3 CLICK the **Keyboard** tab to bring the Keyboard dialog box to the fore.

This dialog box permits changes to the keyboard facility:

StickyKeys
When using the keyboard it is often necessary to hold down two keys simultaneously as, for example, typing a capital letter at the beginning of a sentence. By clicking this check box it is possible to turn the StickyKeys facility on whereby if it is required to use one of the Alt, Ctrl or Shift key in combination with another then a single press of the Alt, Ctrl or Shift key will suffice to hold it down until the second key has been pressed and released.

FilterKeys
This facility permits repeated keystokes with a key held down either to be ignored or to have the repeat rate slowed down sufficiently for the effect of a key held down to be lessened.

ToggleKeys
A toggle key is a switch that is either on or off. For example the Caps Lock key is a toggle key which, when pressed, converts characters entered at the keyboard to upper case characters. It can be very inconvenient to accidently press the Caps Lock key only to look up at the screen to find that the last paragraph has been typed in upper case characters and has to be re-entered in lower case. Using the Toggle key facility it is possible to ensure that high pitched sound is emitted whenever a toggle switch is turned on.

4 COMPLETE this *Activity* with the Accessibility Properties window on display.

Activity 25.2 **Mouse**

1 CLICK the **Mouse** tab to bring the Mouse dialog box to the fore:

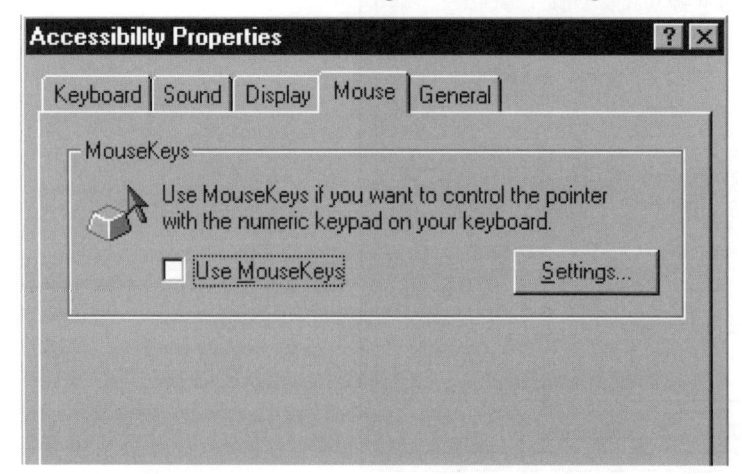

The keyboard can be used to control the movement of the mouse pointer.

2 CLICK the **Settings...** button to view the settings that can be made.

3 CLICK the **Cancel** button to close the Settings for Mouse Keys window.

4 COMPLETE this *Activity* with the Accessibility Properties window on display.

Activity 25.3 Display

1 CLICK the **Display** tab to bring the Display dialog box to the fore.

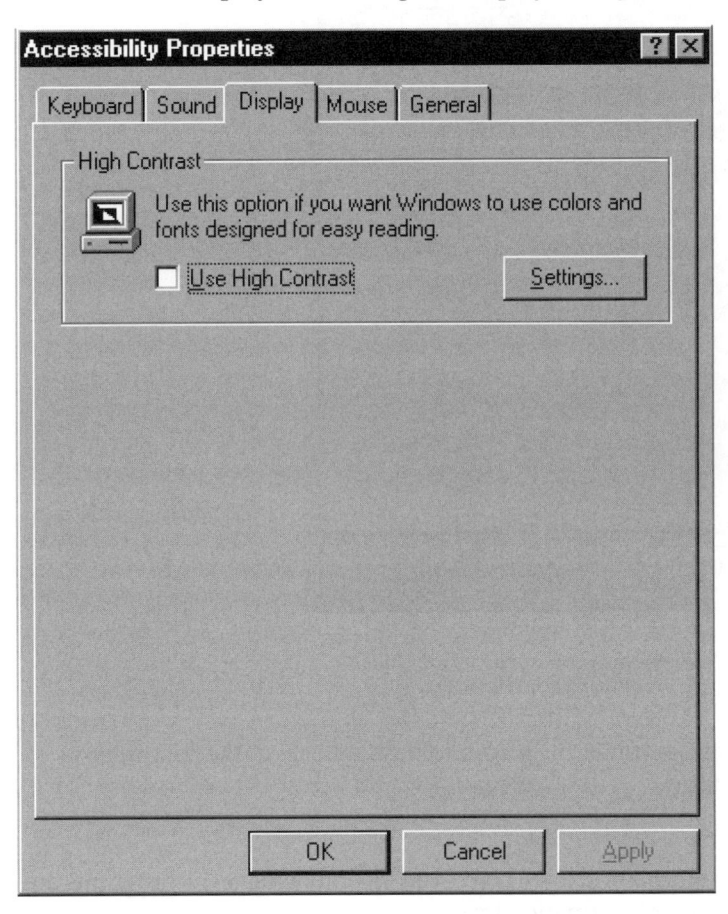

![Accessibility Properties dialog box with Display tab selected, showing High Contrast options]

The screen display can be adjusted to show high contrast of colours and fonts for ease of reading.

2 CLICK the **Settings...** button to view the settings that can be made.

3 CLICK the **Cancel** button to close the Settings for High Contrast window.

4 COMPLETE this *Activity* with the Accessibility Properties window on display.

Activity 25.4 Sound

1 CLICK the **Sound** tab to bing the Sound dialog box to the fore.

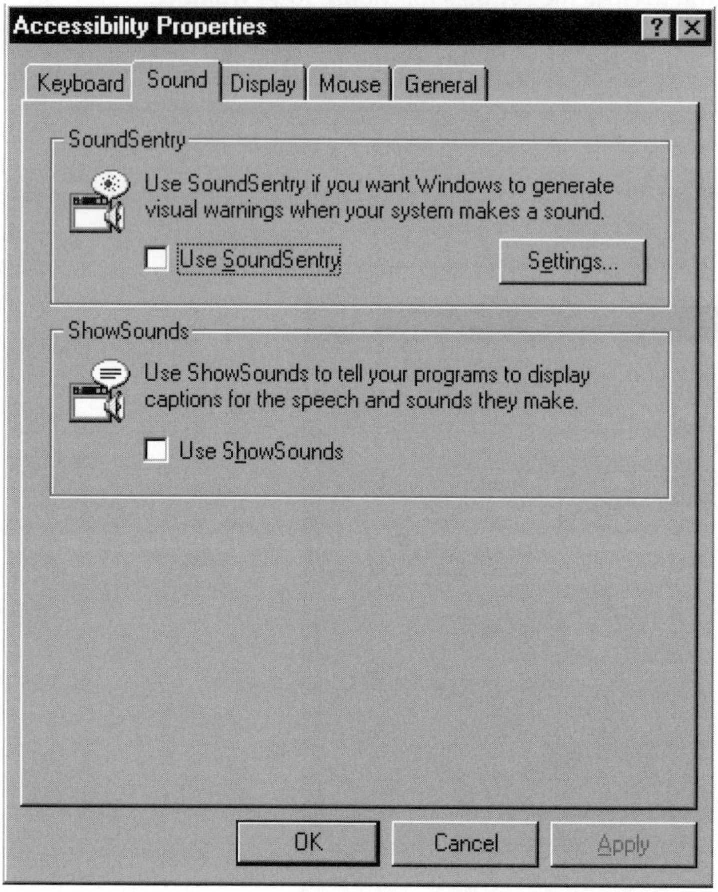

This dialog box has two sections:

SoundSentry
This facility causes a chosen section of the screen to flash whenever the computer's built-in speaker issues a sound.

ShowSound
This facility allows sound information to be conveyed visually whenever programs are used that normally convey their information by sound.

2 CLICK the **Settings...** button to view the settings that can be made to SoundSentry.

3 CLICK the **Cancel** button to close the Settings for Sound window.

4 COMPLETE this *Activity* with the Accessibility Properties window on display.

Activity 25.5 General

1 CLICK the **General** tab to bing the General dialog box to the fore.

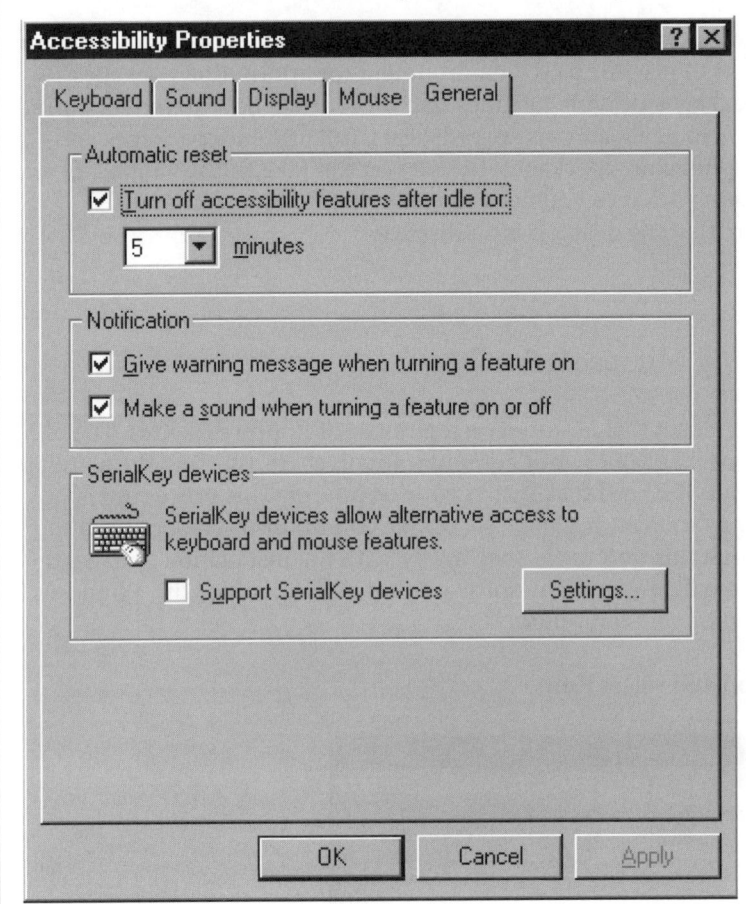

This dialog box has two sections:

Notification
Most of the accessibility features can be turned on or off using a shortcut key. For example, the computer that you are using may be used by more than one person, one of whom may require the accessibility options to be installed. Using a shortcut key enables this situation to be accommodated more easily and avoids the necessity of re-setting the options via the Control panel every time.. Notification settings permit a sound to be issued whenever a shortcut key is turned on or off.

SerialKey devices
This facility permits the installation of an alternative input device for those users who cannot use either a keyboard or a mouse.

| Task 26 | # Installing Microsoft Excel 5.0

> **Installing an application package**

Whilst Windows 95 offers a wide range of computing facilities its main purpose is to provide a GUI environment for application packages. These packages provide facilities that meet needs not catered for by the environment itself, such as spreadsheets, full graphics packages and desktop publishing packages. Before you can take full advantage of an application packages you need to install it onto your computer.

Ensure that the desktop is on display.

Activity 26.1 Installing Microsoft Excel 5.0

Microsoft Excel is a spreadsheet that is stored on a number of floppy diskettes. The process of installing this package onto your computer involves transferring the software on the floppy diskettes onto the hard disk inside your computer. This procedure is performed automatically as soon as you have set up the conditions necessary for it to begin. Furthermore, though this task deals specifically with the installation of Excel the principles laid down here will apply to any software that is compatible with Windows 95 that you wish to install onto your computer.

1 CLICK the **Start** button and select **Run**:

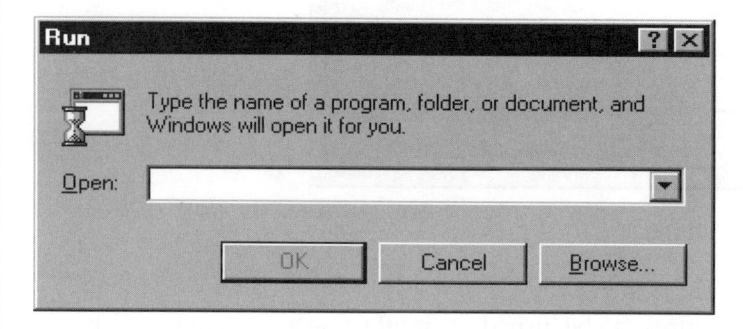

[Run dialog box shown: "Type the name of a program, folder, or document, and Windows will open it for you." with Open: field and OK, Cancel, Browse buttons]

Every installation procedure begins by running a setup file, often named setup.exe where the extension .exe means that the file is executable – it will run when activated. The dialog box that has appeared is asking you where the setup file is located.

2 PLACE the first floppy diskette of the collection containing the microsoft Excel 5.0 files into the external drive A.

3 TYPE into the information panel of the dialog box the name (setup.exe) and location - the A drive:

   A:setup.exe

4 CLICK the **OK** button and immediately the setup file is activated and the opening screen of the installation procedure is displayed:

5 CLICK the OK button to reveal the screen that asks you where you wish all the files to be located on your computer:

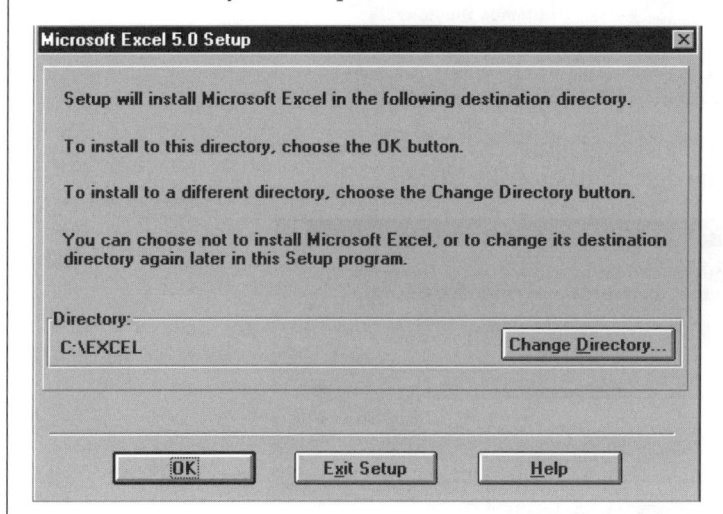

The default location is on the C drive (the hard disk) in a sub-directory called Excel. This is adequate for our purposes.

6 CLICK the **OK** button to reveal a third screen asking you which type of insallation you require depending upon the various options provided by Excel that you wish to have included.

There is a choice of three types of installation:

Typical
This installation is performed automatically and installs the most common options.

Complete/Custom
This installation requires you to tell the computer which specific options you want and which you do not want.

Laptop Minimum
This installation is appropriate to a laptop computer where disk space will probably be at a premium.

7   CLICK the **Typical** button:

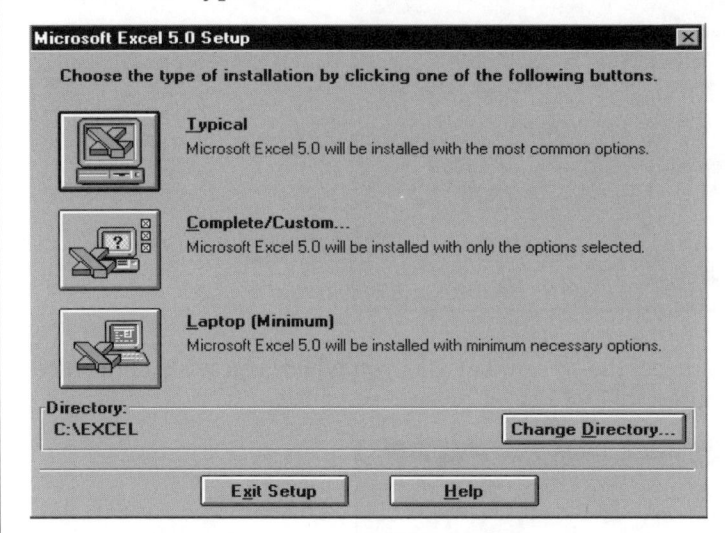

![Microsoft Excel 5.0 Setup dialog showing Typical, Complete/Custom, and Laptop (Minimum) installation options, with Directory C:\EXCEL]

The next screen asks you for the Group name (folder name) in which you wish the files to be placed. We shall accept the default Microsoft Office.

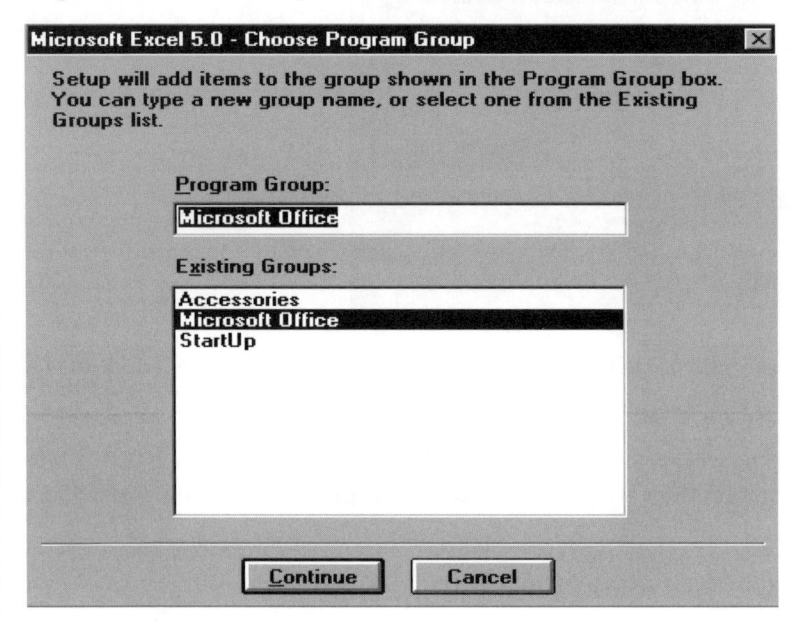

![Microsoft Excel 5.0 - Choose Program Group dialog with Program Group set to Microsoft Office and Existing Groups listing Accessories, Microsoft Office, StartUp]

8   CLICK the Continue button.

The installation procedure continues, prompting you at periodic intervals to change the disk in the A drive. Eventually the installation is complete and you are returned to the desktop where you will see the Microsoft Office folder. Inside the folder is the Excel icon which, by double-clicking, can be activated to enable you to enter the Excel program.

Glossary

Active window	The window that is currently available for data entry. Windows that are open but not active are called inactive windows.
Alphanumeric character	A letter of the alphabet or a numeral.
Application package	A program that is used for a specific application such as a spreadsheet or a wordprocessor.
Background	The screen area behind the active window.
Button	A graphic that is activated to cause a command to be executed by the single click of a mouse.
Check box	A small square graphic that can be selected or de-selected by the single click of a mouse. When selected the check box displays a cross.
Click	The action of pressing and then releasing the mouse button.
Clipboard	A reserved area of memory used for the temporary storage of information that has been copied or cut from an application.
Close	A command which, when activated, will shut down the current application.
Command	A word which can be activated to cause the execution of that procedure described by the word.
Copy	A command which copies selected information in an application to the clipboard.
Cursor	A marker that indicates where the next keyboard stroke will evidence itself on the screen.
Cut	A command which deletes selected of information from an application and places a copy on the clipboard.
Desktop	The screen display of Windows 95 in which all action takes place.
Dialog box	A window that requires information to be entered into it by the user.
Disk drive	A hardware unit that accommodates a disk. The disk is rotated beneath a magnetic head that alternately writes information to the disk or reads information from the disk.
Double-click	Two clicks of the mouse button performed in quick succession.

Drag	The process of moving a graphic across the desktop.
Drag and drop	The process of dragging one graphic to superimpose it over another.
Drop-down menu	A list of commands that appears when a command is clicked.
File	An organized collection of data that is stored either in memory or on a disk under a single filename.
Filename	The name given to a file. It comprises up to eight alphanumeric characters followed by a full stop and then three further (optional) alphanumeric characters.
Font	The design of the type face of the alphanumeric characters.
Graphic	Any element of the Windows 95 display.
Icon	A small graphic that represents an application.
Maximize button	The button at the top right-hand corner of a window which, when clicked, causes the window to expand to occupy the entire desktop.
Menu	A list of optional commands.
Menu bar	The bar containing a list of commands and located beneath the title bar.
Minimize button	The button at the top right-hand corner of a window which, when clicked, causes the window to shrink to its icon.
Object	An amount of data created in one application but embedded in another. The link with the originating application is maintained so that accessing the object causes the originating application to be activated.
Open	A command which, when selected, opens the application in the active window.
Paste	A command which copies the contents of the clipboard to a selected location in an application.
Pixel	The smallest gaphic possible on a computer screen.
Point	The action of causing the pointer to move to a specific location in an application.
Point size	The size of a font, measured in points.
Pointer	The graphic that moves around the desktop by moving the mouse over the worktop.

Radio (option) button	A small circular graphic that can be selected by clicking. When selected the button displays a black dot.
Restore button	The button that replaced the maximize button when a window has been maximized. Clicking the restore button causes the window to shrink to its original size.
Scrap	A file created when part of a document is dragged to the desktop.
Scroll	Ranging through information that will not fit onto the screen in its entirety.
Scroll bars	Bars at the side and bottom of a window that facilitate scrolling.
Select	To highlight a graphic by clicking it and making it ready to respond to the next command.
Task	An open application.
Title bar	The bar at the top of a window containing the name of the application in the window.
Wallpaper	The decorative pattern on the desktop.
Window	A rectangular area of the screen that contains an application.
Wordwrap	The ability for text automatically to run onto the next line of a document without the return key being pressed.
Worktop	The desk over which the mouse is pushed.

Index

Accessibility 119
Accessories 26
Alignment 34
Alt-F4 5
Arrange icons 17
Auto Arrange 17

Backing up files 92
Backspace 30

Calculator 27
Check box 3
Clicking viii
Close button xi
Closing a window 5
Colour palette 43
Colour schemes 104
Commands 2
Comparing files 97
Control panel 15
Copying 32
Creating an object 58
Cursor vii
Cutting 32

Date/Time 15
Dialog box x
Display
    Customizing 100
Display settings 106, 121
Double-clicking 11
Dragging 3
Drawing a diagram 51

Editing a document 39
Editing patterns 102
Embedding an object 59
Excel 5.0 124
Explorer 64

Filenames 64
Files 64
    Accessing 71
    Backing up 92

Comparing 97
Copying 78
Deleting 79
Disposing of 19
Extensions 64
Restoring 95
Searching 89
Find 73, 87
Folder 69, 76
Font 33
Formatting a disk 76

General settings 123
Grid lines 55

Handles 52
Help x, 8, 80
Help contents 83
Highlighting 30

Icons vii
    Arrange 17
    Desktop 14
    Display 100
    Shortcut 15
    Taskbar 22
Insert text 30
Installing software 124
Item list box 105

Keyboard settings 112, 119

Linking an object 61

Manipulating an object 60
Maximize button xi
Menu bar 2
Menu options viii
Minesweeper 4, 13
Minimize button xi
Mouse vii
Mouse settings 114, 120
My computer icon 14
Microsoft Excel 5.0 124

Notepad 72

Object 58
Overwrite text 30

Paint 27, 43, 47, 56
Passwords 109
Pasting 32
Point size 34
Pointer vii
Pointing 3
Print range 42
Printer 41
Printing a document 41
PrintScreen 56

Question mark 81

Radio button x
Re-sizing a window 3
Recycle bin 19
Regional settings 117
Restore button xi
Restoring files 95
Reverse video 30
Ruler 35
Rules of Solitaire patience 9

Saving a document 38, 46
Scrap 84
Screen items 103
Screen saver 107
Shortcut icon 15
Slider bar 49
Solitaire 2, 7, 9, 13
Sound settings 122
Start button viii
Switching between applications 4

Tabbing 36
Task bar viii, 21
    Manipulating 22
Text cursor 29
Text enhancement 32
Text manipulation 33
Title bar x
Tool bar 43, 47
Triple-clicking 33

Wallpaper 101
Warning window 66
WordPad 26, 29, 37, 56

Zoom 53